# KELLY
# HOPPEN
## INTERIORS

To Tash, Sienna, and Savannah, with all my love forever x

# KELLY HOPPEN INTERIORS

Text by Sarah Stewart-Smith

Photographs by Mel Yates

**Rizzoli**
NEW YORK

New York · Paris · London · Milan

# CONTENTS

*Page 1* **THE BEAUTY OF A NEUTRAL SCHEME** lies in the balance of texture, tone, contrast, and light. The Plexiglass lamp with a silk truffle-colored shade is by Porta Romana and ties in with the custom-made purple-glass door handle.

*Page 2* **ORGANICS SUCH AS THIS QUARTZ SECTION** from Ganesh Retreats create a lively textural tension when placed in contrast with sleek blackened oak.

*Opposite* **THE LEATHER DINING-PLATE CHAIR** by Jimmie Martin, at Rhodes W1 restaurant in London, is in cool contrast with the bespoke slatted screen and crystal chandelier by Spina.

First published in the United States of America in 2011 by Rizzoli International Publications, Inc.
300 Park Avenue South
New York, NY 10010
www.rizzoliusa.com

Originally published in the United Kingdom as *Kelly Hoppen Ideas* in 2011 by Jacqui Small,
7 Greenland Street,
London NW1 0ND

Text copyright © 2011 Kelly Hoppen

Photography, design, and layout copyright © 2011 Jacqui Small

2011 2012 2013 2014 / 10 9 8 7 6 5 4 3 2 1

ISBN: 978-0-8478-3575-1

Library of Congress Control Number: 2010932869

Publisher Jacqui Small
Editorial Manager
  Kerenza Swift
Art Director Lawrence Morton
Project Editor Zia Mattocks
Production Peter Colley

Printed in Singapore

# FOREWORD

Kelly has a passion for style with an aesthetic like no other. She is a very dear friend, and for many years I have admired her strength and success. She is a woman with a strong vision, who instinctively combines comfort with contemporary chic.

Fashion, lifestyle, and art are all reflections of our individual personas. Learning how to re-create the visual references that we love is an exciting journey for any homeowner. Kelly has made this achievable for everyone in the pages of her beautiful book, and guides us through her ideas and vision.

*Victoria Beckham*

# INTRODUCTION

I have had more fun writing this book than any other. It is always such an illuminating journey to look back at my work and share all that I have learned. Design is a process that nourishes and talks to all the senses and is as much about practicality and beauty as it is psychology: Design is never just about what you see; it is about what you feel. I can think of nothing worse than a space that is without either the physical feeling or mental sense of comfort.

That I still learn so readily amazes me, and the subtlety of the process is as surprising as it is delightful. My curiosity and determination to experiment, create, and try forever more have never been so pronounced, and the body of work in this book is an illustration of that. While writing this, my lead was to create the "little black book of ideas" of how to get it right for you. More than anything, this book is a

book for you, one that will give you the confidence to design a beautiful, practical, workable home that is tailored to suit your vision of how you want to live.

*Kelly Hoppen Interiors* is my seventh book, and what I have come to know with absolute certainty is that it is the spirit of a home that creates the perfect home in which to live. The single most important message in this book and the one that I have enjoyed learning the most is this: Never underestimate the power of balance and harmony because, once this is deeply rooted in the very foundations of your mind and your home, anything and everything are possible.

**IN MY DINING ROOM,** I am surrounded by collected pieces that I have carried from home to home. Floating shelves—an integral part of my design style—give me endless ways to create and change displays as and when I am in the mood. My dining table is a great example of a Kelly Hoppen signature organic because its solid oak form has a sensuously curving "freehand" edge.

# HOW WE LIVE

EACH OF THE HOMES I HAVE DESIGNED AND LIVED IN HAS BEEN AN ONGOING EXERCISE—AN EXPERIMENT, IF YOU LIKE—WHERE I HAVE TRIED TO UNDERSTAND, MORE THAN ANYTHING ELSE, HOW WE SEE THINGS, WHAT GIVES US CONTENTMENT, AND WHAT WE ARE REALLY TRYING TO ACHIEVE.

**THERE IS SO MUCH MORE** in this home than I have ever had before—a marked shift toward a feminine, luxurious, organic glamour in which I feel very much at ease. There are more objects, more furniture, more texture and subtle contrast, and there is more black-and-white. When I found the vintage polished steel and brass triangular coffee table at one of my favorite antiques shops, Talisman, I knew it was the essential centerpiece for my living room. Mixed with my vintage chairs and a pair of Modenature Chelsea sofas—all reupholstered with damask linen, with fat pillows in silk velvet— the effect is softly chic against the blackened original floorboards, the black glass chimney-breast wall, and the white linen drapes. Treasured favorites such as the bronze Ajoure and lacquer Flibuste Pedestal side tables by Christian Liaigre reappear again and again in my work for their glossy chic, as do vintage objects, black-and-white photography, and great lighting, such as the ceiling-to-floor crystal and silver chain Kelly Light Sculpture that I designed for Spina.

**INCLUSIVE KITCHENS** are the focus of home life and the setting for relaxed entertaining, as well as family meals. Sublime white in many textures sets the tone for this sleek kitchen-dining space, with the glamorous mix of furniture and lighting grounded by the dark oak floors. The roomy kitchen is laid out for optimum practicality, with task light over the island provided by the trio of Hive pendants. For the dining space, I chose acrylic Saturn chairs by Andrew

*How you design your home should never be just about the look*. Your home must work for you and how you live. When I am working with clients, I always try to get to the real psychology beneath the many layers of desire and need. It is my firm belief that you are never going to live properly in a space unless you have uncovered those facets and found the core of what makes you feel good. In essence, your home must represent who you are.

We all have a vision of how we want to live, but rarely do any of us actually look at how we really do live—what we do habitually, what makes us happy, what works with ease, what creates tension. Does your fantasy match up to reality? So, each of us has to look at what we would like against what we need, balanced with what we can afford, and come up with the best possible compromise in order to end up with that good feeling. That sense of contentment is the holy grail of how to live, and it is different for everyone.

If you were to ask me how we live today, I would respond, "How do you create a home that has a life span of ten years, let alone how do we create

## KEY CONSIDERATIONS

▦ How will you accommodate the family?

▦ Identify each family member's needs— ask them to put together a few tear sheets from magazines or books to illustrate their ideas. Everyone, however young, has their version of what makes them feel comfortable.

▦ Ask yourself and the rest of the family how you want to feel in each room in your home.

▦ Talk about your ideas together, so that everyone feels involved.

▦ Avoid buying into someone else's lifestyle. Be yourself and follow your own ideas.

Martin because they are delightful, if unexpected, in combination with the white-painted St. Paul Home trestle table. Circle mirrors give just the right softening contrast to the masculine Kevin Reilly Altar light above the table.

*Living is feeling. And how you want to feel can be reflected in every aspect of your home.*

**IN A LARGE-SCALE OPEN-PLAN SPACE,** creating a feeling of warmth through the well-considered use of materials and furnishings is paramount to engendering a sense of comfort and ease. Defining distinct zones through the layout is also key to the success of the space. In this warm taupe-wood-lined chalet, modern opulence with a hint of old-school grandeur is heightened by way of the layout, scale, textural combinations, and choice of accessories. The Antler Art chandeliers are a dominant feature of the

living area, just as the Ochre horn chandeliers characterize the dining zone. The organic curves of the Promemoria armchair and the ottoman that I designed soften the lines of the architecture and have just enough traditional edge to work within the space.

interiors that are timeless, elegant, and youthful?" An ageless interior can be remolded and gently evolved so that it remains timely and right for the moment at the same time as it serves your needs.

The modern way of living has essentially removed privacy because we have merged our living spaces slowly but surely into a multifunctional communal zone—kitchen, dining room, and living space have become one as we live out our family-centric lives. We have entwined technology into the home, leaving us little separation between work and life, and therefore less chance of downtime and the good feeling of simply being. In effect, we have taken away some of what our grandmothers had put in place in terms of how a home should function—this is not a bad thing because it grew from how we live, but in response I toy with the idea of reintroducing a morning room that is separate, sunny, and playfully informal: a room committed to downtime.

Having recently lived in both a vast lateral loft space and a smaller vertical space, I know that, when it comes to living space, I want a big living room that leads into a kitchen that leads into a dining area that leads into a garden. I want a gym, an enormous dressing room, a bedroom, and a bathroom, and I do not really care whether I have a guest room. You have to ask yourself your own questions based on how you live and with whom, just as I ask these questions of my clients when I design their couture homes.

I live on my own, but what if I decided to live with someone again? If this were the case, these would be the questions to myself: Where will his place be for

**TWO VIEWS** of this warm and welcoming living-dining-cooking space show how to zone a large room without losing the sense of space. Centrally positioned furniture in both the living and dining areas keeps the flow of space free to move through and around it. Here I have used contemporary furniture, such as the Modenature sofas and Promemoria armchair, with vintage pieces, such as the Ball Chair, all in varying textures and tones of linen, a key fabric in all my designs. Mixed with a sisal rug, the linen Luz Interiors suspension light, and the Kevin Reilly floor lamp, the overall effect is friendly and inviting.

## CHECK OFF THOSE BOXES

- You are your own designer, and a "little black book of ideas" will be your safety net for ensuring that you create an environment that best suits your style of living.

- Study your list of needs against your budget, and accept that you will have to compromise. Each and every one of us has to do so.

- You cannot run away from the cost. The cost is the cost.

- Make informed decisions on the basis of your priorities, to find less expensive options and solutions.

him to be by himself? Do we need a pair of adjacent bedrooms to avoid the ills of insomnia or snoring and ensure a good night's sleep? At the very least, I know he will need his own bathroom and dressing room, so that I can retain mine and, therefore, the way I like to function and live.

My observation has been that women want a steady, easy change in their environment, whereas men are happier to be molded into an environment. Women are a bit more risqué in their approach. They are often the multitaskers of the family and therefore have to fulfill a large number of requirements. How do you turn from being a mother into being a wife, a

hostess, a goddess in the bedroom? How do you create and balance all these vignettes in your life?

Just as there are no real rules in design, there are no set rules on how to live. You set your own parameters and make your own decisions, and must communicate how you want to live, first to yourself, then to the people with whom you are living.

Living is feeling. And how you want to feel can be reflected in every aspect of your home, from the practicalities of creating comfort to its simple beauty. Design with a free hand on the basis of what you and your family need because your home is your base, the point from which you jump every day.

**THE SLIDING WOODEN DOOR** (*below*) between this adjoining bathroom and bedroom is extremely subtle, providing privacy when required, but not encroaching into the space. It has been painted to match the custom-made leather headboard, and the soft whites and taupes used throughout create a calming mood. Dressing a bed with tactile fabrics, such as silk velvet, with touches of contrasting natural linen makes it even more inviting.

**THE TWO ZONES** (*opposite*) in this living-dining space are linked by color, tone, texture, and the dark oak parquet flooring. The folding screenlike doors can be used to separate the two spaces, and these tie in with the shelving and its sliding "banner" door that reveals or conceals the TV. The palette is warm, with a pleasing balance between the red swivel Gobbi Club chairs by Dennis Miller and the taupe Velin dining chairs by Christian Liaigre.

# INSPIRATION AND PERSONAL STYLE

I BELIEVE WE ARE ALL CAPABLE OF DESIGN AND ALL "SEE" IN OUR OWN PARTICULAR WAY. LEARNING TO RECOGNIZE WHAT MAKES YOU TICK AND FINDING A WAY TO INCORPORATE THAT INTO YOUR HOME IN SOME FORM IS THE KEY TO SUCCESSFUL DESIGN.

*I find people powerfully inspiring. I literally mean that people inspire the design* and ideas that instinctively come to me as a result of communication and a subsequent understanding of their needs and imagination. I constantly meet people who are as excited as I am about the potential of design to absolutely change lives. It may be me that is effecting the physical and literal change, but in every circumstance, be it an acquaintance, a pupil at my school, or a client, it is the individual who has been the trigger for that change. Nothing is ever more stimulating than the people with whom you come into contact. I am inspired by the way people see, and I create for them on that basis.

I always wanted to be an interior designer. Anyone who has read my other books or magazine features knows this and is familiar with the stories of me as a child, driving my mother to the edge by always moving things around the house. As a teenager, my idea of fun was to visit show homes on the weekend and dream about how I would design them. But from the beginning it was not just the beauty or design that attracted me; it was the ability to see finished spaces perfectly rendered in my mind. That period in my life continues to feed my imagination and creativity, as does the experience of my grandmother's home in South Africa, where

## KELLY'S *TOP PICKS*

**BLACKENED ORIGINAL FLOORBOARDS,** which have tremendous character and make a sleek and practical flooring choice, especially for living rooms

**LOW-LEVEL LIGHTING** that glows softly and is very flattering and calming

**SCULPTURAL DISPLAYS** that can be easily changed to suit your mood

**COLLECTING AND CREATING DISPLAYS** is a form of therapy for me. Floating shelves are a fantastic medium because I can shift and change things around to refreshing effect, and do so frequently. That freedom in itself can be powerfully inspiring. Here, in my dining room, an exquisite play of ceramics, rock crystal, black-and-white photography, and ancient Buddhas forms this display on custom-made taupe shelves.

*Designing a home always comes back to creating for you, for now.*

the inspiration is wrapped up in the memory of the feeling, scent, and rituals of life in that home. There is a limitless source of ideas to explore that can be tailored specifically to any job or for any person. This is the magic of design, where you create for you.

My passion for design is what has made me successful at it. It has been my style both to think and to stand outside the box. I started at just shy of seventeen years old with a kitchen for my father's friend. It was the worst kitchen in history, but,

nonetheless, I had the gumption to do it, and it led to my next job. I learned then that nothing short of utter dedication to the client and their needs would suffice. That passion for the job and the design process has carried me through the design of hundreds of homes—I believe not only that you are only as good as your last job, but also that your last job gets you the next. I live by this and the motto: "Learn from the past, live in the present, and create the future."

When I am teaching at my school, one of the tasks I set the students is to pull fashion pictures from a magazine such as *Harper's Bazaar* or *Vogue*. I ask them to look for fashion images that express how they would like to feel in their home. We use these tear sheets not only as a point of discussion, but also as the springboard for inspiration in creating each of the students' dream living spaces. I use this trick myself and have always pulled images from magazines that spark a concept.

Travel is another form of inestimable inspiration: I have often talked of faraway places as being a trigger for a thought, be it a combination of textures, of colors, or a simple case of layout. Any break or little escape, however, always gives me a renewed sense of awareness. It is always in the last day or so during a break that my mind becomes more focused and I feel as if I am ready to fill up again— these moments can be my most inspired, and they are when I notice every minute detail, from the cut of a suit lapel to the shape of a chimney breast. In some form they all find their way into my work.

The inspiration for my current home came from my love of black-and-white photography: I simply wanted my home to look like an iconic black-and-white artwork, framed and held in balance by form, tone, texture, and light. It has been an extraordinarily positive experience for me and allowed me to experiment freely. Designing a home always comes back to creating for you, for now.

When asked about my personal style, I come back to where I started with "East meets West," the title of my first book and the three words that sum up the core of my style. My passion for the grid formation, where I can visualize everything in its place, and for banners in all the varying forms has always been evident (see pages 60–75). My absolute love of taupe and white, cream, stone, and black has always been a signature (see pages 40–49). But over the

past two decades, this style—my style—has naturally evolved; I now see my work as being much more feminine. It is no less ordered, but it is certainly rounder and more layered with texture.

My automatic state of mind rests at more of a spiritual level than a physical one, and therefore my approach is to emphasize the general feeling rather than the look alone. I have never changed that core foundation of my designs; it supports the surrounding philosophies of my work. Over the years people have questioned how I can take inspiration from a taste or smell, but I say that if you have a memory of a dinner or lunch, or you recall the giant wooden table or the honey at breakfast, that memory is recovered over and over again, and more often than not that memory is not about the specific item, but about the good time. I try to put all of that into a modern interior. I have always felt that there is nothing quite like sitting at a great wooden table with the kids, where everyone is playing and joking, and you have the feeling that you are all there together as a family.

**THE SEATED BUDDHA** (*above*) is a powerfully calming, inspiring, and soulful symbol, and one that I have respected since I began designing. This Buddha, from Fiona Jordan, sits silently against a warm-toned, wood-lined chalet wall.

**THE VINTAGE COFFEE TABLE** (*opposite*) from Talisman, in polished steel and brass, is the absolute central piece of furniture in my living room. Not only do its shape and materials add character to the space, but also it gives me a glossy, sculptural surface for art books, flower displays by John Carter, and the ever-changing arrangement of personal objects, such as the stunning crystal and the curious glass owl that was given to me by a friend.

# KEY EL

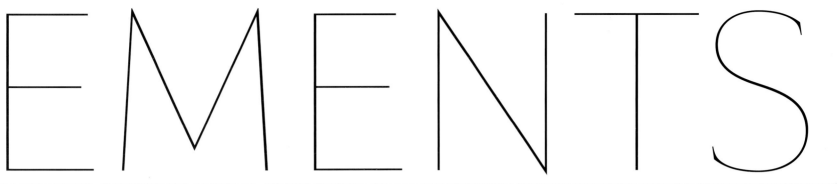

# EMENTS

Texture, form, color, space, light, and balance are the elements that play their part in all my work. Each cannot be separated from the other because they collude in every possible aspect of design—from the sleekest, most modern bathroom to the minute detail in the upholstery of a chair. Texture engenders the life and spirit in a room. Form covers every aspect of shape and surface material. Space is both the space within the architecture and the architecture itself. Light is the magic ingredient, and balance achieves the harmony of mood.

**CRYSTAL CHANDELIERS** by Spina cast magical shadows.

# TEXTURAL PLAY

A FUNDAMENTAL ASPECT OF MY DESIGNS IS THE COMBINING OF DIFFERENT TEXTURES. CHOICES OF MATERIALS, FINISHES, FABRICS, FURNITURE, AND OBJECTS ARE INFORMED BY THE INTERPLAY OF TEXTURE, IN ORDER TO ACHIEVE A PERFECT BALANCE.

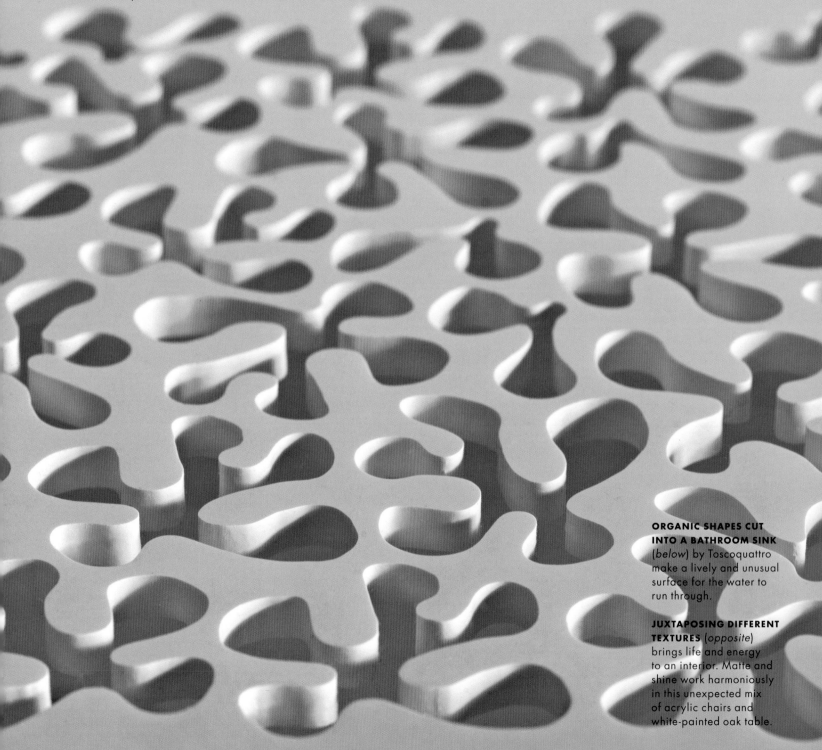

**ORGANIC SHAPES CUT INTO A BATHROOM SINK** (*below*) by Toscoquattro make a lively and unusual surface for the water to run through.

**JUXTAPOSING DIFFERENT TEXTURES** (*opposite*) brings life and energy to an interior. Matte and shine work harmoniously in this unexpected mix of acrylic chairs and white-painted oak table.

*Cashmere, satin, velvet,*
*linen, shagreen, mohair,*
*raw silk, leather,* steel, nickel, glass, oak, stone, marble, ponyskin, grosgrain, mirror, bronze, acrylics, and silver are at once called to mind when I think about texture. This whirl of textural imagery is at the heart of the design process and, for me, is inextricably linked with color, space planning, and lighting. I eat, sleep, and work with texture. I love texture, and it underpins my work on every level because, without it, a neutral scheme will look lifeless.

A mix of taffeta, mother-of-pearl, wool, vellum, bronze, and limestone will be as vital to one scheme as ebony, glass, nickel, and waxed plaster will be pivotal to another. Texture can be as simple as the actual physical feel of an individual piece of fabric, stone, wood, mirror, or metal. Or it can be the layer upon layer upon layer of all the elements in a space, from the furnishings to the objects that together create the overall picture—right down to the minute details of a profusion of spring bulbs in zinc buckets or a band of orange velvet wrapped around a taupe satin pillow. As with color, the skill is in the editing—getting the textural elements in tune with one another, to bring them into balance with your space and your lifestyle.

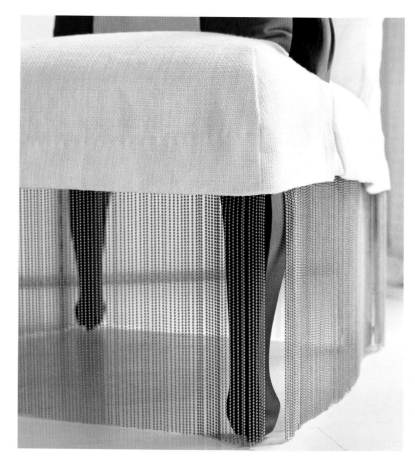

Study texture as you would color, remembering that every aspect of design is wholly affected and enhanced by light, both natural and artificial. The textural shifts throughout a space will be enlivened by the combination of tight and loose weaves, intensified by the mix of shiny and matte, softened by shadow and reflection, but all of this will be magnified to its absolute best by light. Just as texture adds life to color, light adds the finishing layer of textural quality to the whole.

**THE TEXTURAL PLAY** (*left*) between the Monpas metal mesh screen, sheer open-weave drapes, and the blackened hardwood floor is classic Kelly Hoppen.

**UNEXPECTED MIXES** (*above*), such as this classic French bergère chair that I designed, with its linen upholstery and long chain-mail fringe, add a delightful touch to a room.

*Overleaf* **THE EXQUISITE AND DELICATE NATURE** of mother-of-pearl is amplified by setting them as a wide horizontal panel into this curving oak door.

**AN EXCITING TEXTURAL MIX**
brings energy into my living
room, which has reflective
white-waxed plaster walls
and blackened floorboards
with a zebra-skin rug. The
custom-made stairs (installed
by Peter Lind) are carpeted
with a warm taupe silk runner.
The black shutters are from
my own line. More layers of
texture are brought in by my
crystal Kelly Light, the Mark
Brazier-Jones floor lamp, and
the nickel ceiling spots supplied
by Robert Clift Lighting. Fabrics
such as the white voile drapes
with black carpet-tape runner
and the damask linen on the
Modenature sofa offset
glossy surfaces, such as the
lacquered Flibuste tables by
Christian Liaigre.

# TEXTURE KEYNOTES

Texture creates the layers of life and interest within a neutral interior. Actively work to combine matte and shine, rough and smooth, shadow and reflection.

**THIS BESPOKE STOOL** (*opposite*) at Stephen Webster's flagship jewelry store in London is an extraordinarily successful marriage of embossed, skull-patterned snakeskin by Alma Leather and a vintage spun-aluminum base.

**TILE, WOOD, AND METAL** (*above left*) work together to create a beautiful interplay of the horizontal line.

**A SHEEPSKIN RUG** (*left*) overlaid on silk carpet in a room with buttery suede upholstery is pure luxury for both the eye and the skin.

**SPECIALIST STONE-COLORED PLASTERWORK** (*above right*) is in perfect harmony with the ornate velvet-wrapped, vintage mirror frame by Squint and liquidlike crystal-drop chandeliers by Spina.

**SLASHED LINEN** (*right*) at the window of Stephen Webster's store is wildly rock-chic in conjunction with the organic glass Lord Carter chandelier by Mark Brazier-Jones.

# ORGANIC SHAPES AND MATERIALS

FROM THE DOWN-TO-EARTH QUALITY OF WOOD, WITH THE SWIRLING PATTERNING OF ITS GRAIN, TO AMAZING CRYSTAL FORMATIONS AND THE DELICATE BEAUTY OF FLOWERS, NATURAL FORMS AND CURVED EDGES BRING A COMFORTING SOFTNESS TO A HOME.

**GONE WITH THE WIND MAGNIFICENCE** inspired this dramatic spiraling staircase. The oak is a very specific orangey tone and is spectacularly light and contemporary in conjunction with the sensuously shaped wrought-iron railings, so proudly pregnant in form. The staircase flows through two floors, rising fluidly to the ceiling in a swirling meringue shape. It is the kind of staircase you wish you had as a child, with banisters for sliding down at top speed.

**STATEMENT LIGHTS,** such as the bronze Lustre Ovale from Galerie Van der Straeten (*above*) and the Lord Carter chandelier by Mark Brazier-Jones (*opposite*), introduce a vital, fascinating organic quality to a room.

**NATURAL FORMS AND CURVES** (*above and left*) add a softening organic effect, whether the elements are in their inimitable natural form or have been fashioned by craftspeople. I drew the curvaceous lines for the edges of my oak dining table (*above*), which was made by Regal Homes, then repeated the idea for another dining table (*left*). The sleek lines of the Christian Liaigre Velin benches, upholstered in smooth leather, are a perfect foil.

**A MORE GRAPHIC FORM** (*opposite top*) takes its place at Stephen Webster's flagship store, where geometric glass display cases are shaped and placed to form a curve.

**A SECTION OF HARDWOOD** (*opposite bottom*) forms the basis for Jerome Abel Seguin's Kapini wood coffee table. Its presence within the space is both soft due to its natural silken texture and grand due to its sheer size.

*Flowers, leaves, corals, quartz, crystals, and more are picked for their shapes, tones, textures, and unbounded natural qualities.*

*Organic forms are invaluable in the textural layering that informs all of my work.* Organics are essentially natural—from nature—simple and freeform. At the same time, organics are defined by the pureness of a shape, whether a perfect orb fashioned from plastic into a suspended chair, or glass worked into an icy sculpture. Organics have a living freeness that makes them a stimulating element in an interior. They are found, one-off, vintage, plucked from the ground, or have the presence and integrity of being handworked. A sculptural iron light that reads as though it has been sketched into the space by an artist's hand is an organic. Organics are inspiring.

The very process of design is organic to me. I am excited by nature and have always believed that everyday life and the world around us inspire sensational interiors. I have long been as intrigued by the unforgettable shapes created by sinuous rows of rice in a paddy field as I have been fascinated by the veining in marble, the contrast of a flower to its leaf, or the nearly smooth surface of a beach pebble.

# ORGANIC KEYNOTES

Flowers, farmed coral, quartz, wood, and fossils are just a few of the many organics that I combine freely in the textural mix of a contemporary, chic interior.

Organics "shake things up" simply by being what they are, giving a space integrity and intrigue.

**PETRIFIED WOOD BLOCKS** (*above left*) from Bleu Nature—so many millions of years old—have extraordinary depth of texture that is brought out even more in the context of the other materials here—oak, wool, velvet, and horn.

**GLASS AND CRYSTAL** (*left*) of all kinds are favorite textural foils and accessories in any scheme.

**THE DELICACY OF FARMED CORAL** (*above right*)—a fascinating organic form that is so soft, yet rock hard—is emphasized here by the predominantly black surroundings.

**A SCULPTURAL STONE BALL** (*right*) adds to the glorious mix of matte and shine, hard lines and perfect curves, outside in the garden.

**WITH ITS WOMBLIKE SHAPE** (*opposite*), the Bubble Chair has become an iconic organic piece in my work. Here its sensuous curves are at play with the straight lines of the Modenature Arche stools.

I enjoy the imperfect perfection of rough-edged wood. Flowers, leaves, corals, quartz, crystals, and more are picked for their shapes, tones, textures, and unbounded natural qualities. All of these together form what I think of as my signature organics, and I use them freely in the unexpected mix that is my style.

Feng shui teaches us the value of looking after the senses and of living in harmony with nature. It highlights the importance of the elements of water,

earth, metal, fire, and wood, and the way in which those energies flow throughout a home. A tree trunk is very yang, phallic and masculine; a display of grass growing in individual vessels is very yin, soft and feminine. Organics are sensual, comforting, the high notes, the base notes, the subtlety, and the boldness. They mix things up just by being, creating surprise, intrigue, and their own moments of beauty within a space, which in itself is organic.

**A PLAYFUL VIGNETTE**
(*below*) has been created through the juxtaposition of a vintage clock face with a classic Ball Chair. Propped against the wall behind the chair, the clock face reflects the chair's circular shape in a perfect example of lighthearted organic design.

**MODERN GRANDEUR**
(*bottom left and right*) is found in the form of an oak staircase with sensuously curved wrought-iron railings. It rises two stories and is surrounded on one level by a series of vertical oak sections cladding a curving wall and on another by curved oak walls and doors with a mother-of-pearl inlay.

**REMINISCENT OF MULTIPLYING CELLS**
(*above*), this series of circular mirrors by DK Home creates a stunning installation. Repetition of shape or line is very effective, and here a giant pairing of mirrors flanks a kitchen doorway, with a third set in the adjoining room.

# COLOR

I AM KNOWN FOR MY PALETTE OF NEUTRALS— BLACK, WHITE, CREAM, GRAY, AND TAUPE. THESE MAKE THE PERFECT BACKDROP FOR ANY SCHEME.

**SUBTLETY AND CONTRAST** of tone and texture are the keys to a successful monochromatic scheme where neither the black nor the white dominates and there is a natural balance between the two. Adding elements such as the bronze Christian Liaigre Ajoure side table, the wrought-iron Mark Brazier-Jones Sera Lantern floor lamp, and the zebra-skin rug brings highlighting focal points into the design.

*I have always wholeheartedly enjoyed a monochromatic palette.* To my eye, it embraces all the neutral tones between the opposite poles of black and white, plus the black and the white.

This palette has an infinite range of blacks, charcoals, grays, and whites, browns, taupes, sands, and creams. It forms a limitless variety of neutrals that can be put to work with vibrant tones of burnt orange, luxurious purple, earthy green, glorious red, and, sometimes, emperor's yellow. Dwelling on this locks my mind on to the creation of vastly rich, exciting colorscapes that translate into wonderfully workable, comforting homes.

Every one of us sees and responds to color in our own way. When I am putting color together, I always start with a natural linen fabric. Instinctively, I will know whether it is a taupe or a sand tone. If it is gray-brown-based, it belongs in the taupe family; if it is yellow-cream-based, it hangs with the sand group. Brown is not just brown; it can be bitter chocolate or honeyed oatmeal. White can be blue- or umber-based. Just the slightest shift in tone can throw out the whole, or give me the beauty I seek.

I never mix the taupes and the sands together in a scheme. A taupe linen next to a sand linen will look dull. Taupe goes with white, while sand goes with cream. Taupe works best with nickel and other silvers, while sand is in harmony with bronzes and golds. That does not mean that bronze and taupe cannot be mixed, nor does it mean that sand will not work with silver. Metallics and reflective materials can be moved between the families of taupe and sand. Trust your instincts and go with what is beautiful, harmonious, and exciting to you, and mix a signature palette to create a personal colorscape vision.

**A RICH AND SENSUOUS IMPRESSION** (*right*) is given by the combination of the black velvet cushions and the charcoal damask upholstery in conjunction with the lace banding on the white linen pillows. I particularly enjoy this part of the room because the grouping is reinforced by the powerful black-and-white photograph of a woman wearing a sexy lace dress—*Jessica in Lace Dress* by Louise Bobbe.

**BLACK AND WHITE** (*above*) have been used to give this staircase dramatic flair—the wide green band on the drapes balances the weight and depth of contrast.

## IN NEUTRAL

- I cannot separate color from texture. A natural linen in a sleek, glazed finish will look entirely different from a wide, chunky-weave linen in the same color.

- Black, charcoal, dove gray, and silver are as invaluable to me as white, cream, sand, and gold, but I am careful to never mix taupe tones with those of sand because the two are incompatible.

## MONOCHROME PALETTE

I liken the success of a monochromatic palette to that of black-and-white photography, where the serenity of an interior scheme lies in the subtlety and contrast of tone and textural combinations.

### WHAT WORKS WITH *MONOCHROME*

A RANGE OF BLACKS, from purest ebony to charcoal, mixed with whites that can have undertones of gray or taupe

REFLECTIVE SURFACES, such as glossy lacquer or silky polished plaster

CONTRASTING TEXTURES that are surprising and enlivening within the space—such as the combination of linen, lace, and velvet shown here

CRYSTAL LIGHTS for reflection and feng shui

### WHAT DOESN'T WORK WITH *MONOCHROME*

NOTHING—as it goes with everything

# TAUPE PALETTE

Taupe is the most perfect neutral color—
and there are so many tones that
embrace or hover between mushroom
and gray-purple, giving you enormous
design scope within a single palette.
Taupe is neither too warm nor too
cool, so its effect on a scheme is that
of complete harmony and calm.

## WHAT WORKS WITH *TAUPE*

PURE WHITE—paint, plaster,
wood, or fabric

TEXTURAL plaster finishes

BLACK-STAINED WOOD—for flooring
or cabinetry

GLASS—clear, as well as dramatic
accents of green, purple, or red

SILVER OR NICKEL finishes

STONE MATERIALS that have
gray or mocha undertones, such
as slate and gray limestone

A TEXTURAL MIX in the same
taupe tone

## WHAT DOESN'T WORK WITH *TAUPE*

BUTTERY YELLOW TONES in any
material, hard or soft

GOLDEN WOODS, such as oak

TAN LEATHER because it contains
too much yellow

SANDY-COLORED STONES—for
flooring or walls

DARK CREAM CERAMICS or any
accessories that contain any hint
of yellow

**THIS MOOD BOARD**
(*above left*) has been
translated into my
bedroom in London
(*above*). Every tonal
color and material
texture, from the crushed
white silk velvet to the
silvery shag-pile carpet,
is included on the board.

**THE ACCENT OF RICH
MULBERRY RED** (*opposite
above*) in both the rough
texture of the linen pillows
and the smooth texture of
the leather ottoman and
carpet border lifts the taupe
scheme of this living space.
The mood board (*opposite
below*) illustrates the bones
of the design, showing how
it translates into the finished
interior with furniture by
Christian Liaigre.

## PERFECT ACCENTS FOR TAUPE

Taupe is the perfect foil for rich, deep tones, such as mulberry red, purple, burnt orange, and chocolate brown—colors that can be injected into a scheme to lift the palette and delight the eye. Taupe also works as well with bronze as with nickel and chrome, and always works with a pure white accent.

### TAUPE RULES

▮ You can create wonderful interiors using taupe-only materials, as long as you have sufficient texture and contrast between the different elements—mix the rough with the smooth, matte with gloss, opaque with sheer.

▮ A dash of the perfect accent color will enliven the whole space.

▮ Taupe loves clear glass—it is like sun breaking through clouds.

# SAND PALETTE

A sand palette is warm, earthy, comfortable, and natural. Sand is a yellow-based color and has an organic richness of tone that works perfectly in country-style homes. Contemporary designs in sand palettes tend to have a whisper of traditional flair.

## WHAT WORKS WITH *SAND*

THE CONTRAST of white and the easy warmth of cream

SAND-BASED neutral linens and natural buttery suede

ALL TONES of caramel, coffee, toffee, rust, and a touch of orange or yellow

STONES that contain beige, such as French limestone

WARM METALS, such as verdigris, bronze, copper, gold, and brass

MOTHER-OF-PEARL details

NATURAL HONEY-TONED oak flooring

## WHAT DOESN'T WORK WITH *SAND*

ANY TONE of taupe

ANY TYPE of wood with a pinkish base

TOO MUCH black

BLUE-BASED stones

METALS in black or copper tones

**THE COMBINATION OF SUEDE AND LEATHER** in this sand scheme (*far right*) is in perfect pitch with the textures of the white shades and the cream shaggy carpet. The natural white and cream tones in the petrified wood blocks bring in another form of texture that is beautifully peaceful in this wood-lined living space. It is easy to see in the mood board (*right*) how this particular yellow brings in just the right amount of light-handed contrast. The Quinn sofa by Meridiani is covered in linen, and the IPE Cavalli Opium ottomans are upholstered in soft suede. The curving leather Rosetta armchair and Pia hanging light above it are both from Promemoria.

*A sand palette can be put to work with coffee, cream,
toffee, rusts, and the right kind of earthy, organic yellow.*

# COLOR MOMENTS

The introduction of color will overlay a design with chic, wit, warmth, and drama. The right color will lift a neutral scheme, shaking it up to create a new level of impact—either serenely subtle or outrageously bold, depending on the treatment.

**THE QUILTED RED VELVET FABRIC** (*above and opposite*) from Abbott & Boyd used on these Meridiani Belmondo armchairs is the perfect foil to the charcoal grays in the shag-pile carpet and velvet walls. The mood board (*above*) shows the textural play between the materials and how key the red is in relation to the gray tone that has been repeated in different textures and tones. Andrew Martin's steel Alphabet side tables, which spell out "MOVIES," add a final note of sparkle in this home movie theater.

**RICH ORANGE, TAUPE, AND BLACK** (*above*) is a favorite combination of mine because it is harmonious, even though the orange is strong in the space. The mood board (*left*) is one of the simplest I have done, and it illustrates its own quiet strength, which is precisely the feeling I wanted to achieve in this mezzanine library. The vintage, velvet Squint chairs work well with the delicate Bip Bip side tables from Promemoria and Ochre table lamps.

## PERFECTLY ACCENTED

- Gather your neutral palette together first, then add one color at a time to see the effect it has on the rest of the colors and textures. Make a mental note of how the different colors affect your mood.

- Remember that taupe works with whites, silver, and nickel, and any color that is purple-, pink-, or blue-based, such as purple, green, and red.

- Sand works best with warm tones of toffee, bronze, yellow, and orange.

- Black is an excellent accent color in a taupe scheme, while bitter brown is delightful with sandy tones.

# DECORATIVE DISPLAYS

YOU CAN MAKE A DISPLAY FROM ALMOST ANYTHING. A DISPLAY CAN MAKE THE MOST OF A SINGLE BEAUTIFUL PIECE, OR IT CAN BE THE GROUPING OF EVERYDAY ITEMS THAT ARE USED TOGETHER TO REMARKABLE EFFECT.

**A SINGLE QUIRKY ELEMENT** (*below*) such as this crystal and metal lizard wall light—Lézard Électrique by Mathieu Lustrerie—makes a charming decoration, positioned solo in its own space.

**A SIMPLE SERIES OF MOSS BALLS** (*right*) in circular glass vessels makes a strong display because the impression is magnified by the reflection on the surface of the lacquer Continent cabinet by Christian Liaigre. Another pair of identical moss balls is repeated on the Robert Kuo O side table.

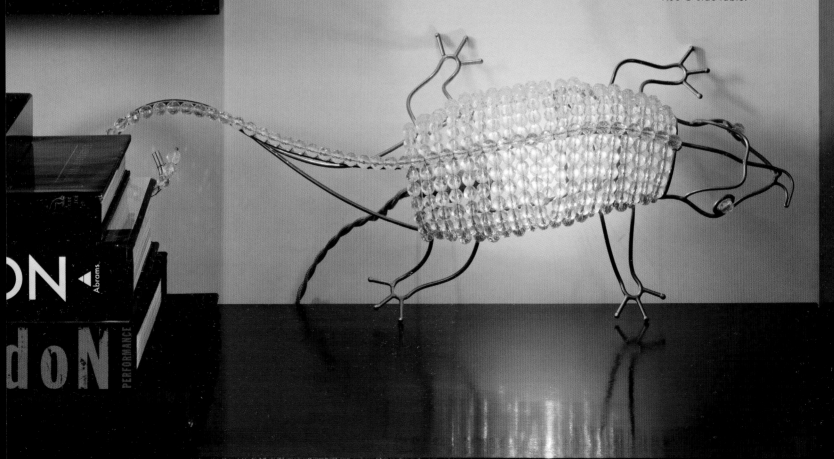

*When you are creating a display, look carefully* at what you own and think about what you would really like to have on display, as opposed to what you have always had out on show. Be excited by the process and, if you are starting from scratch, search the markets and local antiques fairs, and build up some new collections from whatever catches your eye and makes you feel good.

I am known for my rows of goldfish bowls filled with coral, coils of white rope, or sand, which run the length of tables, countertops, and shelves. An arrangement such as this can be strict and linear, but will work equally well freehand and loose, as long as the items are linked in some way (perhaps by color or texture) or belong to the same family. This principle of repetition can be applied to many types of object, whether they be vintage glass, candles, shells, pebbles, or tiny ceramic bowls. The trick is to use a number of like objects together to create a group still life because this will have far more impact than if any one of these individual pieces was left standing on its own.

**THE VINTAGE LACQUER BUFFET** (*opposite*) by Milo Baughman is a 1970s piece that I found at Talisman. It is perfect in my living space for displaying some of my treasured accessories, and it is sublime in conjunction with the photograph *Librario Escuela Julio Mella*, by Desiree Dolron, which I have moved from home to home.

**GLOSSY SURFACES** (*below*) are a magnificent base for silver and glass because they reflect and magnify the textures and forms. A pair of Christian Liaigre Flibuste Pedestal lacquer tables (*left*) and the vintage steel and brass coffee table (*right*) provide excellent display points in my living room for ever-changing vignettes of accessories, books, candles, and flowers.

## THE ART OF DISPLAY

▦ Begin by taking everything away, then edit items you wish to display and store the rest.

▦ There must be a color code or other relationship between the items.

▦ Be very fluid and simple. Put things down and feel whether they are in the right place. Use only items of which you are proud.

▦ Use the impact of repetition when you have many of the same type of piece.

▦ The cardinal sin of display is to create an altar where there are a figure or large object in the center and symmetrical objects on either side. Instead, group two pots with some candles, for example, on one side.

▦ Candles are something that you use and should be lit, not displayed as objects.

▦ Whether using a tabletop or shelf for display, start with the tallest piece on one side, and line up the other pieces in decreasing size.

▦ On a shelf, leaning and overlapping photographs of different sizes will look more interesting than similar-sized pictures lined up in a row. Your mantra is: "Overlay and layer to create depth and interest."

▦ Have two things together side by side, but not at a jaunty angle. You can then add items to bring in different textures—such as a combination of glass, silver, and wood.

▦ Use less—you do not have to fill a space to make it work. A beautiful opaque glass vessel, for example, is enough on its own.

▦ With few objects to display, always work on one side of the surface or shelf.

▦ I always finish arranging and walk away, then look again a few minutes later. I might move something a fraction. I do this one more time, then I know it is done.

▦ Be brave: Your creativity is an expression of you. Move things around every few months, to refresh the look and feel of your home.

Individual artifacts require special consideration. Crowding a unique piece with other elements is an absolute no-no. You want to be able to see it in its own space. The art of calligraphy shows us that it is not the calligraphy itself, but rather the space around the calligraphy that matters—wise words that will help you to have the confidence to leave some things on their own.

One of the reasons I do not hang all my pictures, but choose instead to let some of them lean, is so that I can easily move them around. As a result, I see them in a different light, in a new context. I have always put framed photographs and pictures into displays on shelves. They lean and they overlap, and, positioned as such, they make their own story. Pictures displayed in this way are also an excellent foil for objects and accessories placed in front of and around them. I love that feeling of being able to effect quick changes; few of us change anything, but a home needs to be refreshed, and creating new displays every six months or so is an ideal way of achieving just this.

**NICKEL-CAPPED FLOATING SHELVES** have become a Kelly Hoppen classic, the idea for which came to me as I was putting photos into albums using traditional corner mounts.

*Overleaf* **SPECIALIST PLASTERWORK** by Polidori Barbera has a life of its own. The alcove is lit to display my bronze sculpture— a fabulous vintage find—and white ceramic books.

## SHELVED DISPLAYS KEYNOTES

Elegant floating shelves elevate displays to a higher, "art" level.

Let your displays have breathing space, so that the shelves do not feel crowded on the eye.

Floating shelves work equally well either in contrast to the wall color or finished to match and "disappear."

**BEAUTIFULLY BALANCED SHELVES** (*above left*) illustrate my signature style for displays of overlapping objects and framed photographs.

**BLACKENED CABINETS** (*left*) and floating shelves make for a graphic, stylish moment in this living space. Leaning photographs overlapped with curvy bowls are in wonderful soft contrast with one another.

**CONTEMPORARY, WHITE PORCELAIN EMPEROR FIGURES** (*above right*) in two sizes stand proudly on this ebonized wood shelf that connects to the adjoining architrave and lines up with the wall uplight to create harmonious symmetry.

**VINTAGE BOOKS** (*right*) are fascinating to my eye, and stacked and tied like this they become an art installation in true floating-shelf style.

# U BEGIN

A good beginning starts with a focused mind, and there is no better design practice than that of laying out mood boards to get your vision under way. Seeing your influences pinned to the boards will increase your confidence and skill. Raid fashion and interiors magazines for references—a Chanel jacket can be as key an inspiration as a finished room. Put it all on the mood boards, one or more for each room, leave them for a day, then revisit them with a fresh eye. Do not file swatches and samples away—keep the boards on view because this will move you ever closer to the right design decisions.

**AT WORK IN MY LONDON STUDIO**, where I initiate every design by compiling many mood boards detailing every facet of every room.

# HOW TO PLAN YOUR SPACE

THE LAYOUT OF YOUR HOME IS INTEGRAL TO HOW IT
FUNCTIONS AND HOW IT FEELS, BOTH IN TERMS OF
THE CONFIGURATION OF THE ROOMS, WINDOWS,
AND DOORS, AND IN TERMS OF HOW THE FURNITURE
IS ARRANGED WITHIN EACH SPACE.

*Previous pages* **THE LINES OF THIS LIVING ROOM** have a symmetrical feel, which has been created by the architecture, the custom woodwork within the space, and the folding screen doors. This is reinforced by the strict layout of the Augustin sofas and Flibuste side tables by Christian Liaigre, and the swivel Gobbi Club chairs by Dennis Miller. Even the leather-bordered rug plays its part in keeping the lines of the space true to form and in balance.

**THE GRID IS PERFECTLY ILLUSTRATED** (*left*) in this hallway, where custom woodwork outlines each doorway and makes the space flow freely, while at the same time creating an intriguing view.

*My inbuilt mind map
always comes into play
when I plan space.* I see space in three parts
simultaneously: The *grid* forms the lines of a room and
creates the backdrop, the *zoning* defines its function
and layout, and the *flow* brings the whole together and
creates the movement and mood. It is crucial to
understand space this way because these three
elements work in harmony with one another to give you
the best results you can possibly get from your space.

Available space has to be your first consideration.
How do you want to live in and use the space? Do
you have a clear idea of how you want it to look and
feel? Ask yourself these questions, and write down
your needs and desires.

People are often tempted to go ahead and fill a
space without careful consideration, but I believe it
is hugely advantageous to take the time to examine
space using this type of "mind map." It will enable
you to gain a perspective that will give you greater
freedom and confidence to design for yourself.

A room is made up of six surfaces—the floor,
ceiling, and four walls—and the space contained
within holds natural light. Study and make notes on
the light throughout the day because you need to
know how it fills the room in order to plan your layout.
Natural light and the physical bones of the room are
your starting point.

## Grid forms the lines of a room

To begin, imagine the space in a room on a three-
dimensional grid, so that you can play with and
understand the vertical and horizontal planes. This
grid provides a framework through which you
become aware of how to line up the room. It will
enable you to make a judgment on what will work in
your particular space and give you the beginnings of
its possibilities. For instance, if you want to make a
room appear more horizontal than vertical, deeper
baseboards, chair rails, and picture rails will achieve
this goal. To enhance a sense of height, vertical
panels or tall, slim mirrors draw the eye up.

I often define and divide space with what I call a
"banner" or "runner." This is any contrasting band of
color, fabric, or hard surface that runs up a wall,
around a pillow, over a table, or across a floor. Banners
can be very slim or almost as wide as the room. They
are fantastic for division and definition (see page 74).

It is essential to have floor plans. If you are doing
your own, they must be measured accurately and
drawn up to scale on graph paper. If you are using
an architect's plan, make sure that you check the
scale of the drawing at the outset (to avoid any
chance of misunderstanding, go over it with the
architect or builder prior to committing to anything).

If you are designing multiple rooms in your house,
look at your home as one whole space; imagine
yourself walking fluidly through the existing rooms.
This will help to determine any advantages to
knocking two rooms into one, to create a larger
living-kitchen zone or bed-bathing zone.

**THE KELLY LIGHT
SCULPTURE** (*above*),
made from silver chain,
chrome, and crystal,
was designed by me
for Spina. It falls from
ceiling to floor, casting
an interesting form of
decorative light in my
London living room.
The light also zones the
space, making a clear
distinction between the
landing and the entrance
to the living area.

**THE FLOOR PLAN IN THIS KITCHEN** illustrates how the grid forms the lines and workability of the space. The black-stained oak floors with inlaid poured-resin runners defines the floor space and lines up the room with the windows and the kitchen and dining zones. Even the Mirage Gas Lift bar stools by Danetti are a vital part of the grid lines because they follow and repeat the lines of the room as a whole.

**USING THE GRID** has simplified this SieMatic kitchen to its purest form. The flow of space leads you naturally from the kitchen to the dining area, and vice versa, and the subtle low-level lighting that follows the line of the units further reinforces this, as well as defining the sense of space and adding another layer of texture. Accessories such as the black flute vases draw your eye and soften the lines to just the right effect.

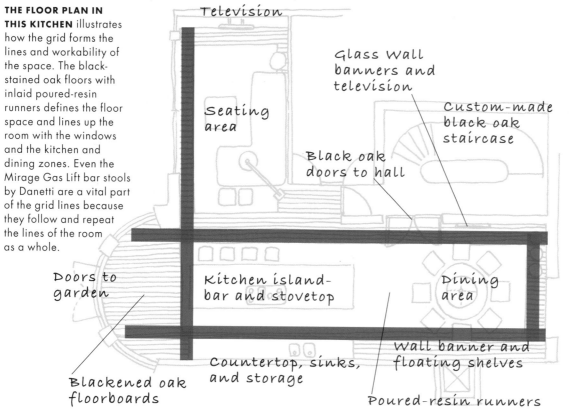

Television

Glass Wall banners and television

Seating area

Custom-made black oak staircase

Black oak doors to hall

Doors to garden

Kitchen island- bar and stovetop

Dining area

Blackened oak floorboards

Countertop, sinks, and storage

Wall banner and floating shelves

Poured-resin runners

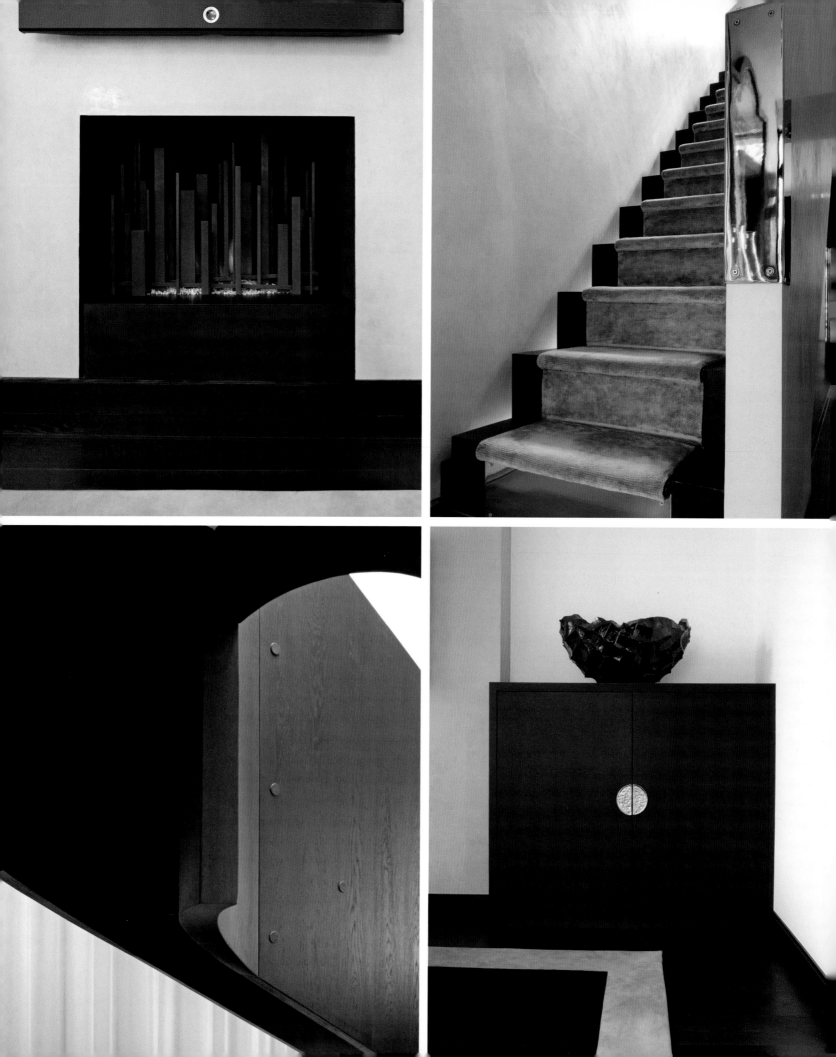

**CRISP LINES OF BLACK** (*opposite, top left*)—in the form of the oak floor, Metropolis fire sculpture by BD Design, and the television screen—keep the flow of space in this room.

**SHADOW-GAP LIGHTING** (*opposite, top right*) at the edges of my staircase in London make the stairwell appear to float. The blackened oak treads and risers are softened by the silk taupe carpet runner and the white-waxed plaster walls by specialists Polidori Barbera.

**CURVES AND MOVEMENT OF LINE** (*opposite, bottom left*) combine to create a powerfully sculptural black oak staircase that is the centerpiece of this London home.

**CUSTOM-MADE CABINETRY** (*opposite, bottom right*) is an important part of designing with the grid. Here a blackened oak cabinet with chrome handles by Xavier Lebée is the holding piece in the corner of this space. The rug, with its contrasting suede border, reinforces the lines of the room, while the black shell bowl from DK Home on the cabinet creates the perfect contrast of matte and shine, straight and round.

**STREAMLINED BESPOKE BOOKCASES** (*above right*) are a vital element in all the homes I design—this example shows how the grid is just as much a part of woodwork design as it is in the rest of the space.

**BANNERS CAN TAKE MANY FORMS** (*right*). This sliding cupboard door in my kitchen brings the lines of the room up vertically into the space in the simplest, most streamlined manner.

Look at the position of the windows, doors, or fireplace, and imagine lining any of these up to another part of the room or area by way of a banner that forms part of the internal architecture (from windows to doors, for example, or to separate one area within a space from another). You could use a banner to define the line between living and dining, showering and bathing, sleeping and dressing. Or the seating area in an open-plan living space could be contained visually by being positioned on a broad ebonized wood banner contained within an otherwise ivory stone floor.

Added internal architecture, such as full-height double doors, can be used to improve the proportions of a room (see Doors, pages 102–9), and often removing a wall altogether creates an entirely new and delightful space.

Think all of this through quietly by yourself because you will then be in a position to find out from the architect or builder whether or not the property can accommodate your ideas. Remember, you are designing for yourself, not for a resale or to impress anyone else (except your partner and children). As you go, keep organized notes and prioritize what you want and need the space or spaces to do.

The point of the grid is to work out whether this list of priorities can be accommodated in the available space. Compromises may have to be made, but often inspiration will arise to meet the need. If you are designing the room from scratch, it is at the grid stage that your builder, architect, or lighting consultant should draw up the lighting scheme (see pages 88–97).

*The grid provides a framework through which you become aware of how to line up the room and enables you to make a judgment on what will work.*

## GRID CHECKLIST

■ Think of the room in a three-dimensional grid formation of walls, ceiling, and floor, to see the space as a whole.

■ The grid provides a framework that will help you to line up the various elements in a room and work out what will be possible in your particular space. It will help you to find the best background solution for the proposed function of the room.

■ Keep organized notes on what you need from and desire in each room as you analyze the space.

■ Make the most of each room's original features and natural light. In a period or older property, it is often better to go with the inherent imperfections than to impose modern, brand-new perfection.

■ The grid will help you to get the interior architecture right—doors, paneling, and additional architectural features, such as floor and wall banners, that divide and define areas.

■ At this point of the process, work out the lighting or instruct your architect or lighting consultant.

■ If you are imagining a wall treatment such as painted paneling or a wall of mirrors, think it through at this stage in relation to what will eventually sit with it. You do not want to end up with a crisscross of confusing lines when you put the furniture, photography, and art into the space.

■ Doors that slide give the illusion of more space.

**THE GRID CONTINUES INTO THE GARDEN** (*above*)—designed here by Chris Moss, with large box balls planted in pots by Atelier Vierkant. The generous-sized bespoke dining table is finished with Lloyd Loom chairs, which bring another layer of texture to the mix.

**LIGHTING ADDS A MAGIC TOUCH** (*below*). Here a horizontal enclosed alcove in the wall of one of the showers at my home displays a backlit collection of treasured farmed corals.

**A VERTICAL WALL RUNNER** (*opposite*) created in specialist plasterwork by Polidori Barbera is a form of simple artwork that sets off the trio of glass vases and Monpas metal screen.

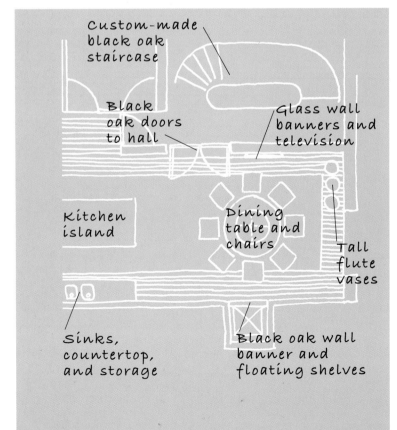

Custom-made
black oak
staircase

Black
oak doors
to hall

Glass wall
banners and
television

Kitchen
island

Dining
table and
chairs

Tall
flute
vases

Sinks,
countertop,
and storage

Black oak wall
banner and
floating shelves

## Zoning defines the function of a room

Zoning defines the room's layout and the way in which you live in it, while allowing free flow and movement through the space. I find it very easy to visualize a space in 3-D, but many people find it tricky. I always present my clients with elevations, to ensure that they can "see" their home accurately and in an assuredly inspired way. If you are at all unsure or believe you cannot visualize your space faithfully, I suggest that you have elevations drawn up despite the expense. This will, in the long term, save on costly or unfortunate errors.

Your floor plan shows you the general zoning—the site of the kitchen, dining area, seating, and so on. Elevations show you every detail for every wall—such as where lights should be positioned and how mirrors, furniture, and chandeliers relate to the wall. On an elevation, you will see all of the items in the correct proportion to the walls, so you will be able to position them in the room with greater skill.

The scale of pieces must be considered at this stage, so all of the existing furniture, mirrors, tables, and lights must be measured accurately and marked up for size on the plan.

Without detailed elevations, the fallback is to go on-site with your floor plan, masking tape and chalk, a tape measure, and the measurements of the furniture and items intended for each room. By marking out each piece in chalk or masking tape on the walls and floors, you will be able to see how the pieces will work in the space. Even with elevation plans, I still occasionally go on-site and mark out the position of furniture because it is a very real exercise that is both focusing and energizing.

The rule at this stage is this: If you are not happy about something, do not go ahead with it. The aim is to make the room fit you like a bespoke suit. Once you have a clear idea of where furniture and other objects will be positioned, mark them accurately on your floor plan.

**THE DESIGN OF THIS DINING ZONE** relates to the beautifully open entrance hallway into which it leads. Smoky glass vertical banners on the wall are in balance with the black lacquer Patsy vases from DK Home and reflected by the single banner in the hallway. I avoid laying out furniture around the edge of a room, preferring to position it in central groups to retain the flow. The display shelves are designed to complement the lines of the room and keep the detail flowing, too. The addition of the porcelain figures is a light finishing touch that draws attention to the horizontal and vertical lines of the space as a whole.

## ZONING CHECKLIST

■ Check off or add to your wish list all the things you want to do in each room, and design with this in mind. It will keep you focused on the outcome. For instance, never build a living-room scheme around the possibility that you will have a big party once a year. Design it to suit you and your family's needs on a daily basis.

■ Begin to zone effectively, so that the space works for you. Ask yourself how you can create an environment that makes you a better person to live with. Try out different options on the floor plan to get the optimum layout for your seating areas, table, and television or computer desk.

■ The scale of furniture and objects is key to the success of any room. If you are working from elevation plans, mark your furniture, mirrors, pictures, and lights on the plans, so that you can see how they relate to the room. If in doubt, or if you are not using elevations, go on-site and mark up the position of all the pieces directly on the walls and floors using chalk or masking tape.

■ Avoid laying out furniture around the edges of a room. You will create a waiting-room effect. Bring the furniture into the space, and place seating together in a group, perhaps grounded and defined by a rug or a contrasting banner inherent in the hard flooring. Ditto for dining areas.

■ Do not try too hard. Be yourself and design for yourself. Your home is a home, not a display house.

**OPEN-PLAN LIVING SPACES THAT FLOW** feel right for both mood and eye. Here there are two seating areas, an intimate zone around a fireplace and a great entertaining space, with an intriguing sculpture by Richard Hoey on the curved wall. The central arrangement of Promemoria furniture keeps access free on both sides. The star organics are the bespoke hanging ball light and Jerome Abel Seguin's hardwood coffee table.

## Flow creates movement and mood

Flow is the movement of space and creates harmony, balance, and mood. Flow pulls it all together because it is not just how you move through and around a space, but also how you respond to it emotionally and how your eye sees it. As with the art of display, just as the space around Chinese calligraphy is as important as the calligraphy itself, the space around furniture and objects in a room is as important as the pieces themselves. It creates "air time"—a room that is not overly full allows movement and flow, which creates harmony within that space.

*Flow is not just how you move through and around a space, but also how you respond to it emotionally and how your eye sees it.*

When working on the flow, your eye should always be given a view—and it should be a good one from whichever angle you look. Think of flow like a fluid wave, and apply this visual to all layouts, whether of a formal dining table, display shelves, and the furniture itself, or of the architectural bones. A good example of this—and I cite this as one of my golden rules—is to apply the same paint color to the internal architectural details, such as baseboards, architraves, and windows, as you choose for the walls. That way, the eye will flow smoothly around the space, and the room will appear less constrained.

Our other senses of sound, touch, and scent are as much a part of flow as sight. I love the analogy of lingerie as applied to a room—just as it is the pretty panties and perfectly fitting bra that define the lines and shape and bring a feeling of chic to an outfit, the "undergarments" of a room provide the structure, which you dress up with furniture and lighting, and accessorize with the jewel-like effect of perfumed candles, flowers, sound, and treasured objects.

**THE FLOW OF SPACE IMPROVES** any room, whatever its size, because flow creates harmony for your eye. Here a giant circular Modenature Reflets mirror creates the illusion of greater light and space, and the tall glass vases planted with palms by floral designer John Carter, the silver Elm chair by Asiatides, and a row of large metal pots all reinforce the effect with their reflective surfaces. The careful use of upscaled objects or furniture in a small space can add to the presence of the room, without making it feel confined.

# FLOW CHECKLIST

- Flow is the movement of and through space and how your eye reads it. It creates the harmony and balance in a room and, ultimately, defines its mood.

- Do your research. For instance, if you look at Japanese interior or garden design, you will see simplicity at work. Study it because it teaches you to give groupings or individual items breathing space and shows how to place things together so that they are in balance with one another.

- Mirrors are magical because they create the illusion of light and space.

- There are many ways to fill a room. It can be done with the right vast piece of art on the wall and a single sofa and light, just as it can with several defined, organized groupings of furniture and walls filled with pictures. If you are in the latter camp and have ten things on the design board, try to bring it down to five. Less is often more.

- Work with all the senses of sight, sound, touch, and scent because they are all an integral part of harmony and balance.

# signature BANNERS

A banner is a fantastic way to divide space and zone a room. It draws the eye, lines up architectural features, and creates flow. It can be wood set into stone, rubber in glass, or stainless steel in plaster. In soft furnishings a contrasting banner can run through bedspreads and around pillows to create stunning linear chic.

This banner of blackened oak set into pale gray stone flooring is a particularly good combination of texture and tone. The satin appearance of the dark wood is accentuated by the smudged softness of the stone on either side of it.

Laying the blackened oak floorboards horizontally into polished gray stone makes an interesting textural contrast in this hall, which leads into a bedroom. The lines of the two spaces are grounded by the banner.

Inlaid oak runs from the main hall through the limestone floor of this powder room and continues straight up the wall, making an excellent backdrop to the Squint mirror and Antonio Lupi sink. The full-height door surround and the door itself give the impression of modern grandeur.

Lighting, too, can be designed to read as a banner. Here custom-made vertical lightboxes have been installed flush within the wood paneling that surrounds a flat-screen television.

The vertical polished-plaster wall runner in this bathroom has an inlaid horizontal banner of brushed stainless steel that pulls the room together and adds another texture.

A sleek colored glass runner, with a cantilevered toilet attached to it, zones this bathing space and makes the toilet a smart feature.

Bespoke pillows and bedspreads such as these, made in a combination of damask and linen fabrics with a contrasting banner of chartreuse velvet running through the pieces, are classic Kelly Hoppen.

The use of red Dalsouple rubber inlaid into the white tiled floor of this chalet bathroom is particularly dramatic because the same color has been continued up the wall behind the bathtub in the form of tiles.

*A banner is any contrasting band of color, fabric, or hard surface that runs up a wall, around a cushion or pillow, over a table, or across a floor.*

# WALLS, CEILINGS, AND FLOORS

THE EXPRESSION "CREATING VISUAL
SURPRISE" IS A FAVORITE OF MINE.
ALL THE MORE SO WHEN REFERRING
TO WALLS, FLOORS, AND CEILINGS;
IT IS ON THESE SURFACES THAT YOU
CAN LET YOUR IMAGINATION LOOSE.

# FINISHES FOR WALLS AND CEILINGS

**I constantly think about new, simple, and clever ways of achieving custom-made finishes because the walls and floors provide by turns the background or foreground of a room, depending on how you design and for what purpose you are designing.**

It is therefore essential that you know exactly what you will be hanging on the walls and placing on the floors before you commit to the finishes for these surfaces. Start the design of the room from the inside out, rather than randomly picking a color or wallpaper for the walls and a wood or stone for the floor, then trying to make everything else fit in with those decisions.

Ceilings do not have to be white. In the right rooms, they can be finished in the same way as the plastered or wood-lined walls. In rooms where you have subtle plastered and painted walls, and if you are not carrying the wall finish to the ceiling, it will look far more modern if you choose a paint that tones exactly with the walls.

WHITE-WAXED PLASTER WALLS for their soft, sensuous appeal

MIXING RAW ORGANIC TEXTURES with sleek modern elements

CREATING VISUAL SURPRISE and textural contrast in the mix of materials

## WALLS CHECKLIST

▦ Know what you are planning to hang on the walls before making a decision on the wall finish, so that the two will not be in conflict.

▦ Perfect plasterwork is an art, so make sure that your building contractor is aware of your expectations and that the builder's finish will be to the right standard for the specialist plasterers.

▦ Ceilings should blend and tone with the wall finish. Too sharp a contrast is not harmonious.

▦ Highly polished or lacquered walls are beautifully reflective and produce that element of surprise and "wow."

## Plaster

One of the chief joys of wall finishes is just how much texture and tone you can bring into play within a space. I love using plaster because it adds its own type of depth to a design. Walls can be designed as a quiet backdrop to an art or photography collection, or as the fascinating textural focal point of the entire room, depending on what type of plaster finish and texture you choose.

Plaster is such a great medium because you can create so many finishes. Specialist plasterwork can be commissioned for the precise look you require, ranging from light vertical or horizontal lines to flowing waves, as well as a range of soft, almost smudged subtle tones of color. I have fallen in love with white-waxed plaster because it appears to be soft and almost creamlike on the wall. It is very much my signature to use large-scale textural pattern in plasterwork as well, and another favorite technique is to create surface texture within the plaster, to give an almost stonelike effect.

*Previous pages, left*
**THE RICH COMBINATION** of black oak floors, matching baseboards, and architraves with muted stonelike plastered walls in this New York apartment entrance is enlivened by both the dark oak frame of the leaning floor mirror and its reflection.

*Previous pages, right*
**RIBBED AND GRIDLIKE,** the textural nature of this specialist plasterwork is carried from the walls to the ceiling, to create a flow of finish throughout this powder room. The artwork, *Rosa "Ferreus"* by Ron van Dongen, provides a soft contrast to the wall finish.

# WALLS AND CEILINGS KEYNOTES

Experiment to create a visual surprise by combining materials, tones, and textures.

Simple is always best. Ceilings can be finished in the same way as the walls or painted, along with the architraves and baseboards, in the same tone of color as the wall finish.

**WHITE-WAXED PLASTER** (*top left*) is a stunning wall treatment that I have used throughout my London home, applied by specialists Polidori Barbera because I love the soft, creamlike finish.

**ARABESCATO STONE** (*top right*) was used on the floor and walls of this bathroom in combination with specialist wall plaster in a toning shade in the sink area. The vanity unit was custom-made for the space in black oak.

**THIS SHOWER AREA** (*left*) has a wood-grain plaster finish outside the shower and a white curving plaster relief inside—the two finishes are divided by the glass shower door.

**SOFT-GRAY PLASTER WALLS** (*right*) are strikingly chic in conjunction with taupe oak floors and the Bombato mirror by Davide Medri, with its mirrored-mosaic frame.

## Wood

A wonderfully versatile material, wood is just as beautiful in its natural planed state as it is when oiled, waxed, lacquered, painted, or gilded. More and more, I have been using wood to fully clad walls and ceilings; whitened softwood planks, for example, give a crisp, contemporary rustic look. Such treatments add an organic, relaxed warmth to a room and are superb in conjunction with both modern and vintage furniture.

Wood walls, whether paneled or laid in varying plank widths, can be painted to soften into your scheme. Entire hallways can be paneled in painted wood with doors to match, so that the space reads as one, with camouflaged cupboards.

I like to expand on the idea of the shoji screen, to create walls of horizontal or vertical wood sections—this is effective both as a screen or as a built-in wall treatment. Another way I use wood is in saunas, where I use two kinds of cedar to create a contrast between the walls and seating (see page 218).

## Tile

The ancient practice of tiling surfaces brings a glamorous, sophisticated edge to any space. Tiles can be gold, silver, mirrored, mother-of-pearl, mosaic, stone, ceramic, glass, or composite. I particularly like both reflective mosaic tiles and roughly textured stone tiles—these are sublime when mixed together in bands or stripes. Each one gives the other a spirited contrast and interest in a room.

Mixing textures this way is particularly important in bathrooms, powder rooms, and steam rooms. Even though these spaces tend to be smaller, they benefit from the same attention to detail as any principal room in the house. If you are having a feature wall of contrasting metallic and matte tiles, keep the ceiling and floor tonal to the walls, so that it does not jar the eye. I have created entire feature walls using a combination of mother-of-pearl and wood, and have had equal success with combinations of mirrored and stone tiles.

**THE SLATTED WOODEN DIVIDING WALL** (*opposite*) at Rhodes W1 restaurant in London is a stunning example of contemporary design and custom-made woodwork. The texture and Eastern feel that it brings to the dining area is in quirky contrast to the chairs by Jimmie Martin, which feature graffiti-decorated leather upholstery.

**THE WALLS OF THIS SKI CHALET** (*left*) have been clad in a warm tone of taupe softwood—a beautiful backdrop to the many other textures and tones of taupe, bronze, and pewter that have been used in the space, as well as for this decorative white mirror from William Stringer. The overall feel of the room is warm, calming, and comfortable.

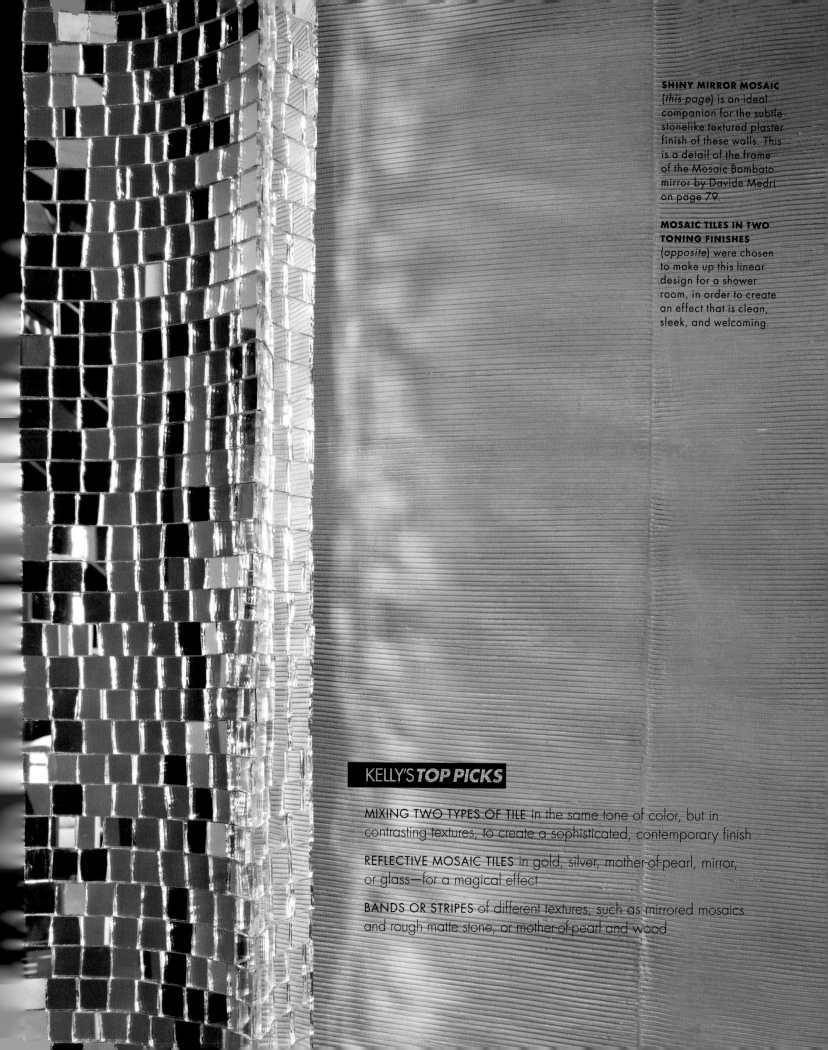

**SHINY MIRROR MOSAIC** (*this page*) is an ideal companion for the subtle stonelike textured plaster finish of these walls. This is a detail of the frame of the Mosaic Bombato mirror by Davide Medri on page 79.

**MOSAIC TILES IN TWO TONING FINISHES** (*opposite*) were chosen to make up this linear design for a shower room, in order to create an effect that is clean, sleek, and welcoming.

## KELLY'S *TOP PICKS*

**MIXING TWO TYPES OF TILE** in the same tone of color, but in contrasting textures, to create a sophisticated, contemporary finish

**REFLECTIVE MOSAIC TILES** in gold, silver, mother-of-pearl, mirror, or glass—for a magical effect

**BANDS OR STRIPES** of different textures, such as mirrored mosaics and rough matte stone, or mother-of-pearl and wood

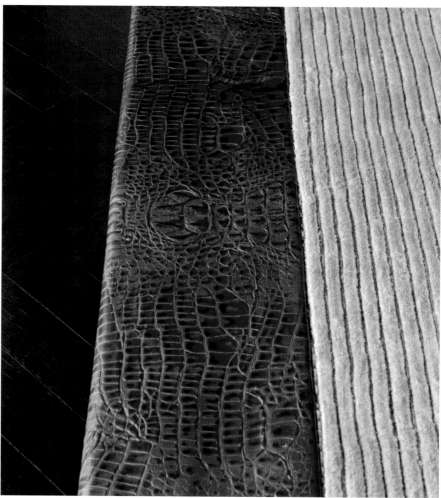

# FLOORING

**The floor is the final textural layer in a design, and it must be timeless and chic, as well as being practical enough to take the wear and tear of daily life.**

I have always loved designing floors, and treat them as artworks because the floor grounds the room and pulls the whole scheme together. For this reason I design the floor last—I have to be sure of each and every other detail in the room, so that I know how all of the elements will gel and work in harmony with one another. Rarely, if ever, will I entertain the possibility of a trendy floor option because floors must be laid to last—reflooring is a highly intrusive and expensive exercise. There are many good materials available to choose from, including reclaimed oak boards, stained hard- and softwoods, concrete, slate, stone, marble, rubber, and glass.

I work with the grid (see page 63) to define zones within open-plan living spaces or to create lines of flow in the form of banners that run along the length or breadth of the floor. The banner can also run up the center of floors in bathrooms, powder rooms, and hallways—this draws your eye to the focal point of a space. The grid is essential to me when working out a floor finish; it is my chance to create contrast in the flooring in both tone and texture—not just in the hard surfaces of, say, the mix of ebonized wood and milk glass, or oak and marble, but also in the rugs that are laid on top.

Rugs are fabulous in every way for the look, warmth, and comfort they add to a room, and all the

**THE JOIN IN THIS ALMA LEATHER FLOOR** (*above left*) has been studded with nickel upholstery tacks. The effect is as though a giant necklace has been strewn across the floor—the perfect design for Stephen Webster's flagship jewelry store.

**SCRUMPTIOUS TEXTURAL DETAIL** (*above*) has been created for this living-room floor in a New York apartment. The ribbed silk rug from Rug Art has been edged with a red embossed leather border by Moore & Giles, and lies on a stunning dark oak parquet floor.

**THE PURPLE BAND OF TEXTURED LEATHER** (*opposite*) on this flat-rib rug from Stark Carpet defines the seating area in this apartment and brings in the crucial element of accent color.

**AN INLAID BLACK OAK BANNER** (*right*) runs through the taupe milk-glass floor of my bathroom, connecting the sink on one side of the room with the bathtub on the other. Reflective milk glass has also been used for the bath surround.

**THE NEAT JOIN** (*below right*) between the black oak and white resin shows the perfection of finish required when flooring materials are combined.

**THE TEXTURAL MIX** (*below*) of the whitened wooden flooring and the pretty lacelike drape fabric is a perfect neutral combination that gives a light, feminine feel.

more so when they have been designed for a specific space. A rug can be made of sea grass, silk, leather, felt, or wool. It can be Persian, Turkish, flatweave, or made with a deep, thick pile.

In many cases, I edge rugs with a wide band of contrasting leather, rubber, or grosgrain webbing. This creates definition, textural contrast, and graphic lines within the space, and it gives me the opportunity to bring in or repeat an accent color, such as purple or red. I particularly like edged silk runners on staircases and shag-pile rugs in bedrooms.

Although wall-to-wall carpeting has been used less often in recent years, in favor of rugs, it can be very luxurious in the right setting. In some homes, for instance, coir matting and old-fashioned Brussels weaves can be the perfect solutions. Choose your carpet or rug textures not only to suit the look of your room, but for its use, too.

## KELLY'S *TOP PICKS*

**USING CONTRASTING** hard materials on a floor, such as stained oak and stone or glass. The laying and joining must be done precisely and on an absolutely solid base to achieve a perfect look.

**SCRUMPTIOUS SILK CARPETS** that feel glorious underfoot

**CREATING A VISUAL SURPRISE** with borders, by way of both color and texture

## FLOORING CHECKLIST

■ Choose a practical flooring material that will work for your space. Stone, wood, and glass are all classic hardwearing options.

■ Stone is an excellent contemporary flooring, but must be sealed to avoid staining. It is best laid over underfloor heating because stone radiates trapped heat (and you avoid cold feet).

■ Wood floors are naturally warm and easy to maintain. They can be resanded when necessary or even painted or stained.

**THE FURNITURE IS GRACEFULLY CONTAINED** within the borders of the rug on the black oak floor in this living space, where I have used a Modenature Domus sofa and chair and Ebene coffee table, with an All I Need daybed from Sé London. The toning taupe suede border on the pale wool rug emphasizes the lines of the room and ties in the floor with the tones of the plaster and unit on the end wall.

**SPARKLING CRYSTAL** (*opposite*) brings a magical dimension to a space, especially when it has been configured into a sculptural design and combined with light. These Tulsa 2 swirling crystal hanging lights from Swarovski make a stunning focal point for a hallway or stairwell.

**DIRECTIONAL CEILING LIGHTS** (*right*), such as these nickel globe-shaped examples from Robert Clift Lighting, are an extremely versatile ingredient of a lighting scheme because they can be used to highlight objects or art, or to wash walls and floors with gentle pools of ambient light.

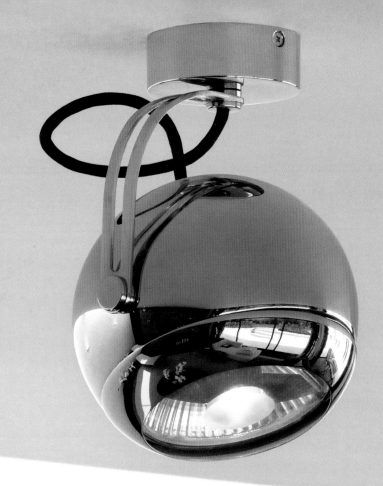

# HOW TO LIGHT YOUR SPACE

LIGHTING WILL NOT ONLY OVERLAY THE DESIGN OF YOUR ROOMS WITH DRAMA AND SUBTLETY, BUT ALSO HAVE A DIRECT BEARING ON YOUR MOOD AND FRAME OF MIND. WELL-LIT ROOMS ARE BY TURNS WELCOMING, CHEERING, SOOTHING, SAFE, SOULFUL, AND SENSUOUS.

*Lighting has to be considered at the very first stages of any project.* It is such an essential design ingredient that it must be given sufficient funds from the budget so that you are able to achieve versatile, flattering light in every room.

I take lighting extremely seriously, using the extraordinary number of light fixtures and light types that are available, as well as creating my own—most notably the crystal Twists and Waterfalls, developed with lighting specialist Robert Clift. I have learned that to create successful lighting, you must achieve a balance of light on all sides of the room. I use different light sources and bulb types to cast light in tones ranging from pure white to yellow, through to blues and soft grays. The three main light sources I like to work with are tungsten, low-voltage, and LED. LEDs are a low-energy low-heat light source that can be used almost anywhere as uplighters, surround lights, floor lights, and shadow-gap lights. The color rendition is very white, but if you use them so that the light bounces back from a soft finish, the effect is far gentler. Soft ambient light is generally created with tungsten bulbs, which produce a warm light; task light is provided by low-voltage directional spots and reading, floor, and table lamps; accent lighting can be achieved using LED strips for uplighting and highlighting wall finishes, fabrics, and artworks.

Downlighters are an essential part of lighting, but be careful how you position them. When installed around the edges of a room, they create a good general light, and some can be directional, aimed at objects or art. Avoid placing downlighters where they will shine directly over someone's head because this exaggerates signs of tiredness. A warm rounded glow that forms a wave of light across a room, in combination with gentle uplighting, is the most flattering form of light, both for you and for the room.

I have had great success with shadow-gap lighting at baseboard level and on either side of staircases. The whiteness of the LEDs along the side of the risers and treads creates the impression of greater width, as well as drawing the eye. Recessed low-voltage lights and LEDs can be installed as floor-washing lights for a soft, low glow. LED linear strips can be concealed within shelving, used within alcoves, and to light cupboard tops, all of which allows the light source to reflect softly back into the room.

**STATEMENT LIGHTS** (*opposite top*) that are beautiful objects in their own right make wonderful additions to a living space. The beauty of this fluidly sculptural wrought-iron Sera Lantern floor lamp by Mark Brazier-Jones is that it looks hand drawn into the space. When lit it casts decorative shadows on the walls and over my collection of treasures and artwork by Desiree Dolron.

**SUBTLETY AND CONTROL** (*opposite bottom*) in lighting is key. In this dining space up-down plaster wall lights, positioned symmetrically on the vertical banners with three tall vases of flowers below each one, glow on the wall. The lighting strip beneath the custom-made floating stone shelf provides another layer of soft background lighting.

**THE JOY OF THIS ARRANGEMENT** (*right*) is not only the combination of the custom-made crystal chandelier with the velvet and Novasuede Villa sofa from Donghia, but also that the chandelier has been suspended so that it hangs where you would expect to see a table lamp. A series of crystal chandeliers, also made by the contractor, each hang at different heights through the stairwell, adding drama and glamour to the space.

## LIGHTING CHECKLIST

▨ The secret of good lighting is to have three or four circuits in each room, so that you can vary the light throughout the day and for different functions. Design for options and control.

▨ Use dimmers or a preset system, so that you can have a "wow" setting for evenings, a comfortable scene for day-to-day life, a sexy nighttime scene, and a bright scene for cleaning.

▨ Often it is best to position pendants and chandeliers over a table or grouping of furniture to the side of a room, rather than in the center, because this casts a welcoming pool of light.

## Layers of Light

Start a lighting scheme by assessing the natural light on sunny and overcast days, and take photographs as a reminder of how the light falls in the room. Refer to the list you made of everything you will be doing in the room. Check your floor plan for the positioning of furniture, which must be worked out prior to the lighting design. Draw up elevations of every wall, showing where pictures, star pieces, or collections will be placed. Pay attention to wall finishes and floors because you want the lighting to bring out their best qualities. Sufficient floor sockets for lamps are essential.

**FOR MY LIVING ROOM** (*right*), I chose the softest of low-level lighting, to subtly enrich the many matte and glossy textures at play—the black glass and white-waxed plaster walls, dark wood floor, sheer linen drapes, damask linen Modenature sofas, polished steel and brass coffee table, and lacquer and bronze side tables by Christian Liaigre. It is the perfect light to make anyone look and feel good, and is glamorous and soothing.

**DECORATIVE LIGHT** The crystal and metal lizard lamp by Mathieu Lustrerie is both pretty and quirky.

**ATMOSPHERIC LIGHT** The warm glow of firelight and candlelight can never be underestimated.

**SCULPTURAL LIGHTS** The two chrome table lamps are stunning vintage pieces that look as fabulous unlit as they do lit.

**CEILING LIGHTS** The directional nickel ceiling lights wash the walls with gentle background light and highlight artworks.

**STATEMENT LIGHT** The Kelly Light Sculpture is an intriguing ceiling-to-floor silver chain and crystal piece that I designed for Spina.

## LIGHTING KEYNOTES

I recommend having a five-amp circuit for table lamps, floor lamps, and task lighting; a circuit for recess lighting that highlights artwork and wall finishes; a circuit for low-level or shadow-gap lighting; a circuit for wall lights and chandeliers; and an optional circuit to light built-in furniture.

**A STATEMENT PIECE** (*opposite, far left*), such as this Lustre Ovale pendant from Galerie Van der Straeten, is very much a part of the welcome wow aspect of this New York entrance hall. Hanging centrally above the cream lacquered table with antique-copper conical base by Robert Kuo, it illuminates the artwork *I Am Not a Geisha*, by Daniel Kelly and casts patterns of light and shadow on the ceiling.

**THE DRAMATIC ARCHITECTURAL QUALITY** (*left*) of this modern staircase is perfectly balanced by the Swarovski Tusla 2 hanging light, specially made to hang through all three stories of this London townhouse.

**A SERIES OF FOUR NICKEL GLOBE TASK LIGHTS** (*right*) hangs above the cooking island-cum-breakfast bar in my kitchen, with additional nickel globe ceiling lights bouncing soft, balanced light into the space.

# signature
# LIGHTS

The quality of light is one aspect of lighting; the actual lights themselves are quite another. I look for star pieces or have them made specially. A star piece might be an extraordinary sculptural chandelier, contemporary flame-shaped wall lights, or vintage metal floor lamps. I scout for one-off pieces all the time. I prize them because they are unique, and always accommodate such treasures in my work. Make sure that you have enough light sockets, and position them to work within the layout of furniture. This is particularly important in living rooms, where you will want lamps on either side of sofas and dedicated reading areas within the room.

The crystal, silver chain, and chrome Kelly Light Sculpture makes a stunning decorative feature in any space. The lights hang full length from ceiling to floor and can be used to divide and zone space, as well as to light it. Beside the light is a photograph of Jibby Beane by Nadav Kander, which enhances the glamorous mood.

Holly Hunt's handblown clear glass pendant lights are beautifully simple and chic. They work brilliantly hung low in a line along the length of a dining table or above a work counter or kitchen island, to provide task lighting.

Wall lights are especially practical in corridors and on stairs. This up-down plaster wall light from Robert Clift Lighting has been combined with low-level floor-wash lights in a hallway, to create my preferred soft, subtle light.

A quirky alabaster wall light with marbled shade from Tindle Lighting produces soft, diffuse light that washes the white wall with a gentle glow. This is a great way to bring subtle background lighting into a room.

These bronzed brass Liberty floor lamps from Estro, with black painted shades, have beautiful flow of movement in their shape, which brings a sculptural element to the room and a utilitarian yet elegant feel. They work well as reading lights in a seating area.

IPE Cavalli's textural metallic wall light is an unusual example. The perforated metal mesh shade on a polished metal plate—reminiscent of a cheese grater—emits small points of light.

Mark Brazier-Jones's ornamental Sera wall lanterns, made from filigree ironwork and glass, are like extraordinary pieces of jewelry, and cast pretty decorative shadows up the walls of this staircase.

This bronzed Man 3 floor lamp from Porta Romana is chicly organic and sensuously sculptural— a contemporary take on a classic standard lamp that works particularly well in a living room, study, or library.

This pendant light from Holly Hunt is a modern twist on a traditional lantern. The handblown glass shade held within a framework of blackened steel encloses a cylinder of stainless-steel mesh, so that the bulb within emits a soft, warm glow.

# PRACTICALITIES

BRINGING A DESIGN TO FRUITION IS A COMPLEX PROCESS, AND IT IS ONE THAT MUST BE CAREFULLY THOUGHT THROUGH WITH REGARD TO EACH AND EVERY DETAIL OF THE DESIGN, THE BUDGET, AND THE WORKS.

*As your own designer, you will also be your own project manager,* and you have to make the time to ensure that things run smoothly, on schedule, and, in principle, on budget. I cannot state it strongly enough: You must be controlled and organized because I can guarantee that if you are not paying attention and are not on-site daily, the result will be the wrong floor finish, a door that crashes into a wall panel, or chrome faucets instead of nickel. Some lapses will be easy to fix, but others will add to the time and cost of the job.

## Mood boards

The purpose of mood boards is to enable you to see the story of your room or home coming together as you add and subtract the various elements. If you are working for yourself, you must create mood boards for every room; they will be both an inspiration and a way of showing you whether you are doing something wrong. An essential part of the planning process, they are also an excellent way of costing your ideas.

**THE VITALLY IMPORTANT MOOD BOARD** (*below*) is the first step in bringing your vision into being. This is where you put your ideas, building this representation of your design to the point where every element in the room is shown either photographically or with samples of the relevant fabrics and finishes. Group the elements as they will be in the actual space, as I have done here: All the lighting is together, the chair styles are together, and, on the right of the board, the combination of seating and accessories is shown. This gives you an immediate impression, which leads to greater clarity and confidence as you refine the design.

For each project I work on, I lay everything out on a series of mood boards. I look at them again the next day and wonder whether what I have put together is really what I want. I rate the process of creating mood boards highly because, once you see images, colors, and textures together, they are lodged in your mind and, without you necessarily realizing it, the core of the idea is also in your subconscious and you really begin visualizing and using your imagination.

Committing fabrics, flooring, furniture, lighting, and accessories to mood boards focuses your mind. To begin with, you can make up an inspirational board of your ideas using cuttings from magazines and furniture brochures, fabrics, and other surface materials—this will show you what you want, and mine often contain fashion images that convey a look or feeling. Just as you lay out your clothes to see how they look before getting dressed, you are laying out the design for a room or home on a board. Eventually you will have a series of finely tuned mood boards for each room. I tell my students that having stacks of paper and cuttings filed away in folders is a bad idea because you cannot see them. With each element pinned to a board, you can readily see how all the various components work together as an idea, both from a glance and up close.

Use the mood boards to cost your idea. On a separate sheet of paper, write down every item on the mood board and work out the figures. For instance, in the kitchen, you have a hit list of oven, stovetop, backsplash, sink, faucets, water filter, and so on. There might be flooring, walling, air conditioning, and doors, and you cost them and perhaps gawk at the price, before reconsidering your options. With your priorities in mind, you begin constructing another mood board detailing the actual elements.

The professional inspiration boards that I put together for every project can make or break a potential job. It is my role as the designer to put the client at ease with me and with my proposed ideas. The one sure way to achieve that is to produce phenomenal boards that not only show the look of the idea, but also convey the feeling and attitude of the spaces, as well as the cost.

**Budget**

The single most important factor of budgeting a project is that you will need more money than you think. A contingency fund of about 20 percent on top of the budget should be set aside for unknowns, such as a structural fault or late delivery of goods. Changing your mind after the event is the single most expensive mistake you can make, so be focused and be sure.

The core works—lighting, flooring, sanitary ware, kitchen, plumbing—always take the bulk of the budget. From the outset, you must cost in the furniture, fabrics, art, and accessories that you want in each room because, however beautiful the shell, it will fail you if you end up living in a half-finished home. Look carefully at what you think you want, and find ways of making savings against an expensive purchase. It is crucial that you be honest with yourself about how much the project will cost.

**Builders and contractors**

Give yourself plenty of time to find the right building contractors and craftspeople. Recommendations from friends are good, but, if you find a construction firm that gives you the right feeling, ask to see a recent project of theirs, visit the property, and speak to their client for feedback. Always ask more than one contractor to bid because this keeps prices

## PRINCIPLES OF THE PROCESS

■ The strip-out and clearing of the site

■ Demolition and removal of walls, if required

■ Structural first fix on building works, including new openings, stud walls, and brickwork

■ First fix for electrical wiring and plumbing

■ Second fix for building works, such as plastering

■ Woodwork, such as architraves, baseboards, and wooden floors, installed

■ Second fix for electrical and plumbing work, including the lighting and the kitchen and bathroom suites

■ Built-in specialist storage, such as shelves, cupboards, and closets

■ Decoration

■ Installation of carpets, drapery, furniture, and soft furnishings

competitive and gives you solid comparisons for cost and time. It is not always advantageous to choose the cheapest quote—you want a proper standard of work and that will be reflected in the price.

Make sure that the contractor's schedule fits with yours. Next, draw up a schedule of works together that lists the individual jobs within the project, so that each floor and baseboard is specified and every electrical outlet is in place. Your contractor will work out the timing for each stage of the project.

Communication between you and your building contractor is key. For instance, arrange fixed weekly meetings in addition to your daily visits. Keep separate but identical files of fixtures and materials for you and the contractor, so that you are both clear on the actual items you require. Check all lead times for delivery at the point of order. Expensive items that turn up early will either get in the way or, worse, be damaged. Who will take deliveries and do a quality check? Of course, there are moments of luck, good and bad, in any project, but the smooth running and ultimate success of a project are always results of good, clear planning.

Moving from room to room should be as much of a delightful, unexpected experience as the rooms themselves. Every home has halls and corridors, and I treat their design like calling cards. You have one chance at making a first impression, and this is the lasting impression. Equally, every time you come home, you want to feel uplifted and happy. The halls, corridors, and stairs are a bit like what underwear is to an outfit—the structural core that sets the "shape" and tone for the rest of the house.

**THIS IMPOSING STAIRCASE** curls up and around to the second floor landing, where it meets a wall of oak inlaid with a horizontal band of mother-of-pearl. Delicate crystals have been formed into a bold cutting-edge light installation, which was custom-made to hang down the middle of the stairwell.

# DOORS

SOME DOORS ARE DESIGNED TO MAKE A STATEMENT. OTHERS ARE THERE TO SHUT OUT THE WORLD. MANY ARE CRAFTED SO THAT THEY DISAPPEAR INTO THEIR SURROUNDINGS. MOST MAKE A FEATURE IN THE HOUSE.

*Above all, a door is a defining element in a space.* It is like a piece of art because a door opens up and takes you into a new experience. When you are designing a door, ask yourself what its purpose is. Where is it, and how important is it?

I see doors as statements that are integral to the flow of architecture, not mere necessities—you have to have them, yes, but they deserve particular attention. Front doors are such a vital part of the architecture of a home and crucial to the initial impact. I think of doors as fabulous scaled-up panels against the wall. They are excellent architectural elements on which to play with textural contrast, especially in a home where there are no original doors or if you have a house or apartment with few architectural features. Given the choice, I replace conventionally sized doors with much taller ones; where possible I take the door right up to the ceiling, particularly in low rooms. This expands the sense of space and dramatically changes the proportions of a room for the better.

The entrance hall is a neutral space. It is there for everyone to see and to share. It creates the first impression. In the entrance of my house, I have a pair of double-width, full-height, dark-stained-wood

**DOOR HANDLES** (*opposite, top left and right*) are to the door what shoes and a purse are to an outfit. Xavier Lebée's half-circle nickel door handles are the perfect match for this grand, white, double front door with a slate door surround. Good exterior lighting is essential; here both the downlights and up-down wall lights were supplied by Robert Clift Lighting.

**LARGE-SCALE NICKEL NUMBERS** (*opposite, bottom left*), together with an oversized nickel mailbox, make a dramatic statement on this glossy black-painted townhouse door.

**A CONTEMPORARY TWIST** (*opposite, bottom right*) on traditional metal door studwork was used on the door to Rhodes W1 restaurant in London.

sliding doors with extraordinary inset nickel handles, which open into the kitchen. It is a narrow house, and creating the opening with these doors was an excellent solution to giving the impression of a wider space. With mirrors and black-and-white photography, the space alludes to the attitude and atmosphere of the rest of the house and welcomes you to my world.

Some doors are designed to be discreet. Most of the doors I design make a statement, however, whether subtle or dramatic. For me, designing doors is about playing with depth and perspective, tone, texture, and interest. Doors are not only about wood and glass; they can also be mirrored or clad with leather, fabric, or paper. Doors can be plastered or inlaid with marquetry. They can be paneled vertically to imbue a sense of exoticism, made as traditional shoji screens, or designed to be all but hidden.

Doors can mimic the materials—wood and lacquer, for instance—used elsewhere in a house, so that there is continuity throughout. It is the same principle as choosing complementary shoes and handbags—you opt for the connection and harmony between the elements.

## KELLY'S *TOP PICKS*

A DOOR that allows you to make an entrance

UPSCALED DOOR HANDLES and numbers that are in proportion to the door and its surround

INTRICATE DETAILING, such as paneling or studwork

**SLIDING DOORS**

(*opposite*) make the most of the space in the entrance hallway that leads into the kitchen of my London home. I designed the blackened oak doors to flow from floor to ceiling, increasing the sense of space, and each has a streamlined bespoke nickel handle. The doors, along with the black shutters from my own line, are in striking contrast with the Altro poured-resin floor by Industrial Flooring and the specialist white-waxed plasterwork by Polidori Barbera. Bottom right shows the hallway with the doors closed; on the left is the view into the kitchen; top right shows the corner of the breakfast bar, with a glimpse of one of the mirrors in the hall beyond.

There are many ways to build a door. It can pivot, rotate, fold, or slide. The available space and the function of the door will be a deciding factor, but first let your mind run with the possibilities.

A door has an obvious function, but it is also an elegant backdrop to furniture and paintings, as well as a hint of what might be beyond. You can gain inspiration from architecture all over the world. You can form an idea from a memory of paintings, photographs, and objects, or the imagination may be triggered by a beautiful Hermès belt with its stitching and aged buckle. All of it can translate into an idea or detail for a door.

Screens, too, are a form of door, and I often design cupboard fronts as screens. Mine are based on Japanese architecture, which is very important to me. I have screens made up that fold in front of one another so they take up the smallest amount of space.

Screens can be constructed to form room dividers that zone and define rooms. I think of them as

**CUSTOM FOLDING DOORS** (*left*) between the kitchen and living area of this London townhouse create a strong screenlike architectural feature and allow you to close or open up the space according to mood and use. The half-circle silver metal door handles are by Xavier Lebée.

**IN THIS POWDER ROOM**
(*far left*), a Japanese-style
slatted screen door with
"enclosed" slats gives
privacy, while still
retaining the same "open"
architectural door and
architrave detailing that
runs throughout the rest
of the first floor of this
New York apartment.

**THIS BLACKENED OAK
SLIDING DOOR** (*left*),
with a subtle matching
handle, has been set
into a deep recess
between a bedroom
and the hallway.

freestanding doors—whether they are opaque,
semitransparent, or "open" in their design, such as
my Circles screen—because they hold you in or lead
you farther into another space. They can be made
from glass, wood, framed fabric, or paper and sheet
fretwork in wood or metal. A screen can provide
privacy or be built in a slatted shutter style, so that
you can not only glimpse a view beyond and feel
connected to the rest of the space, but also enjoy the
beauty of light filtering through the slats.

Screens do not have to be full height—you could
have several at different heights in glass, stone,
specialist paintwork, and leather. It would make the
space feel like a multilayered cubist painting.

Doors and screens are points of focus—the new
fireplaces, the new chimney breasts—the places
where you can introduce something exciting,
dynamic, and unexpected.

**SLATTED SLIDING DOORS**
(*opposite*) look light and
delicate within a space.
These elegant doors are
based on Japanese shoji
screens and are made in
blackened oak. They can
be closed, to separate
the dining zone from the
living area, creating a
more intimate space and
forming a textural "wall."

**OAK VENEER DOORS**
(*right*) leading off the
entrance hall in this sleek
New York apartment are
all custom-made and have
deep matching architrave
surrounds. The lacquer-
topped copper table is
by Robert Kuo and the
bronze Lustre Ovale light
above it is from Galerie
Van der Straeten.

# signature DOOR FURNITURE

KELLY'S DETAILS

Door handles are to the door what earrings are to the face—a finishing touch that will add elegance, chic, grandeur, surprise, and beauty. Most of the door handles I use are custom-made, with an emphasis on textural contrast, shape, and proportion, but there are so many off-the-shelf handles in steel, nickel, bronze, wrought iron, brass, Plexiglass, faceted glass, leather, rope, and wood. I design many of the door handles for my projects to reflect my banners—such as oblongs of brushed steel set flush in black-stained wood doors—and also choose a shape that reflects the lines of the woodwork.

The square lines of this gray wood cabinetry are reflected by the square metal knobs from Haute Déco, chosen as much for their perfect square shape and tone of gray as for the depth that the handle projects from the surface of the door.

I often design door handles so that I can effectively achieve the right solution. These door plates, made by the contractor, have a beautiful patina in the metal surface that contrasts in just the right way with the black oak doors.

The smooth but grainy honey-colored oak used for the cabinets in this dressing room required an equally textural door handle to finish the design. These push-pull, silver, metal, shagreen-textured handles were made by Xavier Lebée.

Sometimes a surprising or eclectic choice works best. I enjoy the delicacy of these horn handles by Ochre not only for their organic edge, but also for how they work on these modern cupboard doors.

I wanted an almost smudged kind of subtlety for the design of these cupboard door handles. The contractor made them from patinated bronze, which works beautifully with the veneered oak.

Often a surprising material or color will add just the right finishing touch to a design. This custom-made purple, faceted, glass door handle is an excellent example of this.

Every detail matters, particularly on finishing touches—Xavier Lebée's Bagatelle handles make an almost perfect circle when the doors are closed, but are still beautifully interesting when separated to form two semicircular handles.

The delicious combination of bleached wood cupboards and bubbly Champagne-glass pull knobs from Haute Déco illustrates how subtlety of color with texture works.

Adding textured handles to smooth doors is highly appealing because the rough texture enlivens the smooth, while the smooth texture tempers the rough. These silvered metal Nomade pull plates by Xavier Lebée are stunning against the black oak.

Simplicity is a key aspect of good design, and here the contractor was asked to create sleek blackened oak handles that would work almost seamlessly with these screenlike shoji doors.

A local joiner made these bronze flush recess handles for a series of whitened wood cupboards in a London townhouse.

The dominant textures in this dressing room are the oak of the cupboards with their horizontal shagreen banners—a beautiful mix. The Xavier Lebée handle chosen to finish the look is a silver metal D-handle, with a shagreen texture within the surface.

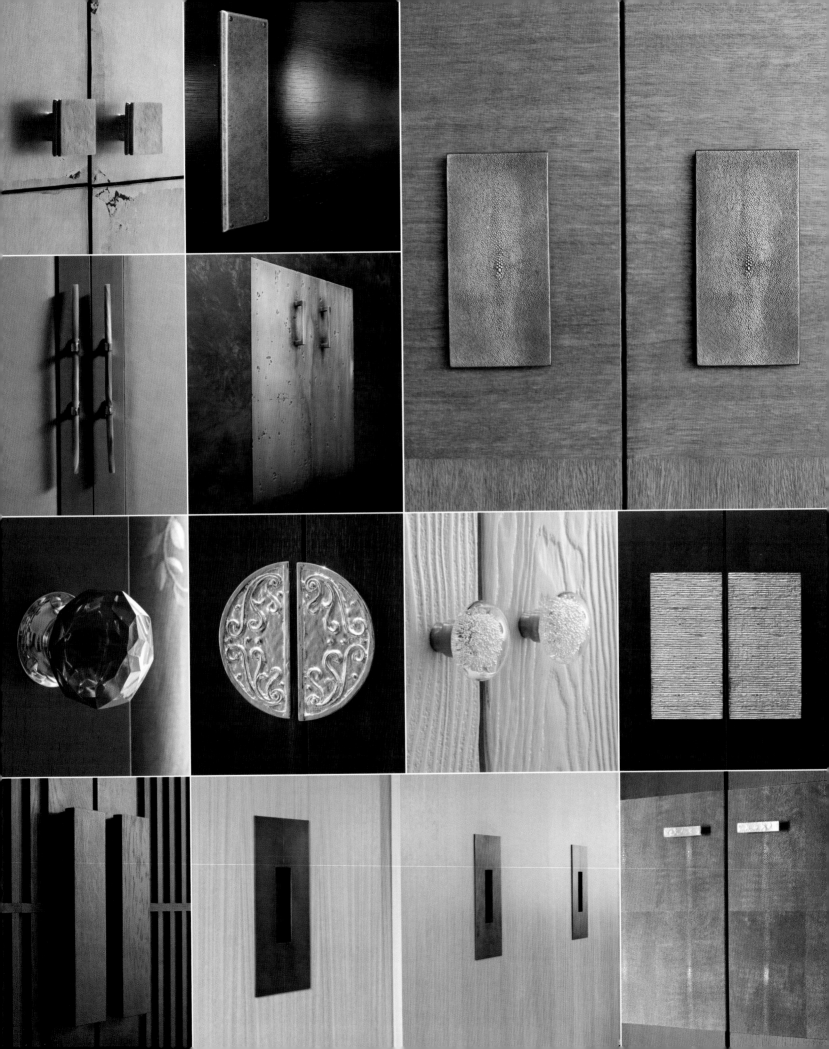

# HALLS

NOT ONLY IS THE ENTRANCE HALL THE WELCOME INTO A HOME, BUT IT SETS THE STANDARD AND MOOD FOR THE REST OF THE HOUSE AS WELL.

*Entrance halls create that first crucial impression.* When I come home, I look forward to experiencing the sense of well-being that my hall engenders. That feeling is what you are designing for—the excited sense of homecoming. First impressions are lasting ones, and you do not get a second chance to make them.

When you are designing, look at your home as a whole space, and imagine moving through and around it fluidly. Think about whether you are having wood or stone flooring, where this flooring leads, and how it will work in conjunction with other rooms because ultimately all rooms lead off the entrance hall. There must be flow and continuity between spaces to create harmony.

Your hall is your hall, so use what you have and make the absolute best of it with well-planned lighting and attention to detail. The hall must be practical—with a shelf or console for keys, bags, and purses, and closets for shoes and coats—but do always bring in that element of display with mirrors, flowers, and objects. This is key to obtaining the wow factor.

**SLIM FLOATING DISPLAY SHELVES** (*left*) do not intrude into this hallway, and the lighting underneath bounces off the polished wood floor, enhancing natural light. Colorful art by Nobuyoshi Araki lifts the monochromatic palette. A Promemoria Pierre stool is perfect for removing shoes.

**THIS ENTRANCE HALL** (*opposite*) is a beautiful example of yin and yang in perfect balance. A Lustre Ovale bronze chandelier commissioned from Galerie Van der Straeten is suspended over a circular copper and lacquer table by Robert Kuo. The dark stained oak mirror on the silver-leaf wall reflects the space, increasing its size and emphasizing the strict masculine architecture, while giving glimpses of the rooms beyond.

**A TEXTURAL FEAST** (*right*) in this chalet hallway includes wood-clad walls of horizontally laid planks in play with highly polished marble floors, gilt leaf-shaped vessels, and a figurative stone sculpture. The effect draws the eye toward the main living spaces. Light plays a crucial role in this design because the entrance hall is on the basement—this lighting scheme sets off infinite reflections, giving the space dynamic energy despite the lack of natural light.

**THE ENTRANCE HALLWAY** (*opposite*) in my London home makes me smile every time I come home. The 1960s zinc mirrors from Philip Thomas are perfect for the space, striking just the right note of glamour. The long, slim double shelf allows me to display an ever-changing scene of flowers and objects. They are overlaid this way because the house is in a crescent, and this was a great solution to disguising the curvature in the architecture. Nickel capping on the corners are a signature feature of the house—it is both highly practical and chic. The poured-resin flooring runs throughout the first floor.

## HALLMARKERS

- Design for the wow factor, as well as for practicality; a hallway gives the first impression of the interior of your home.

- Create continuity of floor finishes, so that your rooms will flow harmoniously from one into the other.

- I have exterior doormats, but you can inset a black coir mat within the hall flooring inside the entrance if you wish.

**THE ENTRANCE HALL** of this historical period house, where little could be changed because of legal restrictions, has been thoroughly modernized with a black-and-white palette, and centered and defined by placing a section of black oak within the Thassos white marble floor. The Monpas table provides the ideal spot for an impactful flower arrangement. The rest of the space is simply and beautifully finished with white-painted walls and three Pearl pendants with crystal drops from CTO Lighting.

# CORRIDORS

**The roads through your home are not places where you spend long stretches of time, but you do use them constantly, so their design is no less important than that of the rooms themselves. They are the linking spaces, so your design choices—materials, finishes, lighting, and furnishings—should be in keeping with the overall feel of your house.**

As with entrance halls, remember to keep the flow of floor finishes harmonious throughout because corridors link rooms to rooms. Work with, not against, the architecture of your home, and make much of textural contrast in your choice of materials and finishes.

The grid (see page 63) will be enormously helpful when you design the doorways and doors and in how you finish baseboards—in corridors they can be effectively matched to either the walls or floor.

I approach the lighting design for corridors as I would for any other space, in order to make the most

**THE BEAUTY OF THIS SPACE** (*above*) lies in the tone of color and the almost metallic textural quality of the plaster walls in conjunction with the marble floor and giant Shield plant pot from DK Home, a bronze sculpture in its own right. The rectangular niche built into the curved wall creates a yin-yang balance and a perfect display point.

**A BLACK-AND-WHITE PALETTE** (*above right*) maximizes the architectural lines of this corridor. A run of identically framed photographs continues the graphic quality of the space, where everything is white except for the doors, door surrounds, and framing. Discreet lighting at low and high levels creates a soft wave of light throughout.

of them, because often there is little, if any, natural light. Low-level lighting that throws light to the floors, then bounces up into the corridor is particularly inviting and beautiful, as well as flattering.

Corridors are spaces, not just roads through the house—sculpture, objects, star pieces of furniture, and pictures can all be used to give these spaces personality and charm. Do not be surprised by how just one well-judged vessel with beautiful flowers or a plant can transform a corridor from feeling unloved into being warm and full of life.

**LIGHT WELLS IN CORRIDORS** are the ultimate luxury because the quality of light in the space is superb—pure, white, clean, and fresh. Here a soft-gray oak floor with matching baseboards expands the width of the corridor. A trio of tall, sculptural bronze plant pots makes an impressive installation and adds an organic flavor to the otherwise slick and modern space.

**THREE VIEWS OF A DRAMATIC STAIRWELL** in a London townhouse show the purity and power of the grid, in action with texture and clever lighting by Robert Clift. The walls and staircase sidings have been finished with white-waxed plaster by Polidori Barbera. This is one of the most difficult pure white finishes to achieve, but one that has incredible warmth and subtlety, especially in conjunction with black-stained oak. The shadow-gap lighting is a new departure for me. Using these LED recessed strip lights makes the steps appear to float, and also visually widens the space. The silk carpet runner has toning leather binding, which adds to the sense of luxury. The success of this staircase rests on the crispness of line balanced by the curviness of the Swarovski Tulsa 2 spiral crystal chandelier that hangs through three floors, ending just above a simply shaped console table by Megaron and a small oval ottoman from Christopher Guy in the hallway below.

# STAIRS

STAIRS ARE A VITAL AND CENTRAL
PART OF THE ARCHITECTURE OF
A HOUSE. THEY ARE RIGHT IN
THE MIDDLE OF THE BUILDING
AND ABSOLUTELY PIVOTAL TO
THE HEART AND SOUL OF A HOME.
A STAIRCASE BALANCES A HOUSE'S
PROPORTIONS, SO IT MUST NEVER
BE IGNORED OR TREATED MERELY
AS A NECESSITY OF FUNCTION.

## STAIRS KEYNOTES

A new sculptural staircase will completely transform a space and create architectural drama, but even very simple treatments produce stunning effects.

**THIS EBONY-STAINED OAK STAIRCASE** (*left*) leads from the first floor to the basement of my home. A glass side panel keeps the look open and modern, so that the stairs almost appear to float. The roundness of the antique Indian stone planters has a surprising and sensuous effect.

**THIS SIMPLE TREATMENT** (*above right*) is timelessly modern, with wall-to-wall charcoal carpet on the stairs and landings. Low-level lighting, boxed banisters, and black shutters from my line keep the look clean and strong.

**STAIRCASES IN SOME BUILDINGS** (*right*) cannot be removed because of restrictions on changes to historical buildings, so I added ebony-stained hardwood edging to the side of this staircase, with a matching handrail. The landings were also stained ebony, while the walls were kept white for contrast and balance. The taupe silk runner adds softness to the palette, as well as comfort. Low-level lighting gives an essential glow at nighttime.

**THIS STAIRCASE** (*left*) was taken to a new level by replacing the spindles and banister with a boxed side capped with nickel. The steps have been painted, and an edged runner flows up the stairs, held in place with nickel stair rods.

*A staircase
is not something
you can miss.
It is the main
sculpture of the house,* the freestanding piece that can take all manner of treatments. Often, however, particularly in historical or period buildings, your options are limited by having to retain the historic features of the home, but in some cases you can create a new staircase from scratch or redo an existing stairwell with astonishing and extraordinary results.

For many people, installing a new staircase is simply not an option; however, in cases where you are stripping out your home, it is well worth considering what dramatic architectural effects can be achieved by designing a new staircase that will completely change the look of your home—the examples in this book illustrate this perfectly. Stairs can be designed to wind up and down in a circular fashion or be more linear and float in the space. Either way, glass balustrades on the landings are a good option because they allows you to retain that sense of openness and flow of space.

**KELLY'S *TOP PICKS***

CREATING NEW and dramatic sculptural staircases that will completely transform the look and feel of the space

CURVES, glass, and openness to enhance a feeling of space and retain a sense of flow

TRANSFORMING the staircase into the star item of a home, whether old or new

There is so much to say about staircases, but the most crucial point is that a completely new staircase must be kept under the aegis of an architect. You simply cannot consider undertaking any work on stairs without professional expertise because the design and engineering are highly complex. One of the main aspects of staircase design that needs to be overcome is that of finding craftspeople who can make custom-made staircases because they are true labors of both skill and love.

If you are considering making major changes to your stairs, make sure that your ideas work with your budget—the worst thing you can do is a "half job." There are many treatments for existing staircases that are both affordable and beautiful, and are far more worthy than compromising a new design. If I were given the choice of having new bathrooms or a new staircase, however, I would take the staircase every time because I could always go back and do the bathrooms at a later date.

There are so many ways of turning an existing staircase into a piece that looks bespoke or, at the very least, like an extremely well-designed part of the home. Carefully think through your ideas, and do some research by looking at architectural sites on the Internet, as well as in interiors and architectural magazines because you will do your stairs only once.

**THIS CURVING STAIRCASE** leading to a bedroom in an old apartment block is a triumph of tone and shape. With taupe wooden steps, a matching indented handrail, and a glass balustrade at the landing, it could not be more restrained or subtle.

**SCULPTURAL SPLENDOR—**I think of this staircase in a London townhouse as whipped cream in black wood. It is by turns organic, sculptural, modern, and effortlessly bold—and it has been the pièce de résistance of my work so far. My aim was to achieve an incredible sculpture, the construction of which was utterly perfect. The wood grains are exquisitely rendered and "move" seamlessly around the staircase, and the undercarriage is just as beautiful as the top. The stairs have been finished with a silk carpet runner and oh-so-subtle integral lighting, designed by Robert Clift, within the recessed handrail.

In buildings that are not subject to restrictions because they are not historically significant, it is relatively easy to change banisters and handrails. The most effective way is to "box" the banister and create a half-height siding to the stairs. This can be finished to match the walls, increasing the sense of space and making the house feel sharp and modern. For another look, treads and risers can be reclad with dark wood or stone, or you can stain the existing softwood steps.

In a historical or period home where you cannot change the staircase, you can still redo the spindles and stain the handrail to ebony, which will refresh and update the look. The work must be done to the highest standards for it to look sleek and loved.

There is a lot to be admired in a painted staircase that has contrasting treads and risers. Equally beautiful is a staircase that has been finished with silk carpeting. My preferred treatment, where appropriate to the design of the staircase, is to carpet the stairs with a runner that has a contrasting band along its edge. More and more, I use silk carpets on stairs because it makes running up and down them more comfortable and less noisy. If I can, I install lighting on the edges—either set into the walls at low level or recessed on either side of the steps—because this makes all the difference between a good and a great end result.

**THE STAIRCASE IN MY LONDON HOME** (*this page*) runs seamlessly through the house, keeping the monochromatic, photographic quality in play, even on every landing, where there are display vignettes. I love the shadow-gap lighting, and use it again and again because its wonderful effect makes the steps, covered with the taupe silk runner that is essential for comfort, appear to float.

I have introduced nickel capping on all the corners, an idea inspired by photographic corner mounts. I also finished the first riser with a nickel kick plate—both practical and sleek. The crystal Kelly Light Sculpture provides a separation between the stairs and living room.

**THIS ARCHITECTURAL STAIRCASE** (*right*) was designed to be very square, very open, and very masculine. The ski chalet is a beauty, with its wood and exposed beams, and this new staircase is a reflection of that character. It is in the middle of the two main living spaces, which meant that it had to blend with everything else while still being a centerpiece. I did not want to compromise on the view to the living rooms, so the design is very open. It is made from taupe-stained hardwoods, but I added Dalsouple rubber treads because I knew that everyone, especially the children, would be running up and down the stairs without shoes, both before and after skiing.

*A staircase is the main sculpture of the house, the freestanding piece that can take all manner of treatments.*

# KITCHENS

IN RECENT YEARS THE KITCHEN HAS BECOME AN
ALL-EMBRACING AREA FOR FAMILY AND SOCIAL
LIFE, WHERE SPACES ARE OPENED UP INTO ONE
ANOTHER AND WE ALL ENDEAVOR TO LIVE MORE
COMMUNALLY AND FREELY.

**THIS OPEN-PLAN KITCHEN-DINING SPACE** flows smoothly into the living area through a pair of black oak folding doors. The dark wood floor, too, flows between the spaces, increasing the sense of openness. The mix of furniture and lighting is so refreshing—the wild curve on the DK Home white bench is exciting and energetic, especially in combination with the acrylic dining chairs, elegant Conciluce glass suspension lights, and Kevin Reilly's Altar light.

*The way we look at kitchen design is markedly different from how we viewed it ten years ago.*

The influences of celebrity chefs, such as Jamie Oliver and Gordon Ramsay, along with cable channels and Web sites dedicated to food and cooking have shifted our perceptions of life in the kitchen possibly more than any other factors. We have been inspired once again to loosen up and cook with abandon. To cook and entertain at home is cool, and this, combined with the aspiration for open-plan living, has made the kitchen a sophisticated cutting-edge environment of ease and beauty, with space for living, dining, playing, and working. It is the theater at the heart of the home, where you relax, tackle homework, and make plans. It is also the place where, if you were invited to supper, you would think twice about turning up in your sweats.

## Kitchen planning

I treat the subject of kitchens as being highly personal and specific. One of my jobs is to deprogram and then reprogram my clients' brains, so that, first of all, they agree to put their kitchen in the right place. The position of a kitchen should always be based on your way of living, rather than on where the kitchen is currently sited, irrespective of whether or not you have to reroute the plumbing. Work on the basis of available space and how you want to use the kitchen. Ask yourself questions and make a list of your needs,

**THE POWER OF SIMPLE DESIGN** (*above left*) is perfectly illustrated by this streamlined white lacquer SieMatic kitchen with blackened wood flooring. Integral lighting is key—the strips of light underneath the units and in the recess above them wash a soft glow onto the floor and ceiling, respectively, making the units appear to float. Downlights in the ceiling provide the task lighting.

**THE KITCHEN BAR** (*top right*) is often the most sociable spot in the house, and I always try to incorporate one in my designs. This island is positioned beneath a skylight, which floods the room with natural light. These Angus Macrae bar stools suit the space perfectly, and the three DK Home Hive pendants add an organic element.

**A WHITE RESIN RUNNER** (*above right*) set within the blackened wood floor defines the bar area in this kitchen and grounds the Danetti Mirage stools.

*The kitchen has become a sophisticated cutting-edge environment of ease and beauty, with space for living, dining, playing, and working.*

**MONOCHROMATIC KITCHENS** are particularly chic. This smart scheme is enlivened by the organically curved oak table built to my design by Regal Homes. The comfortable benches are upholstered in white faux-leather. Non-Random Lights, designed by Bertjan Pot to direct the light downward, hang over the dining table, while Robert Clift Lighting supplied the nickel ceiling spots—which bounce light into the space above the units—and the pendant lights suspended over the island, which provide the task lighting.

**THE GLASS-TOPPED ISLAND IN MY KITCHEN** (*above and right*) was set with a four-ring gas stovetop. It is a triumph for me because the rings are arranged in a single row, so that I never have to lean across a hot pan. Across the island, the open sliding doors frame the way into the entrance hall of my home, where I have a vignette of two stunning zinc-framed 1960s mirrors from Philip Thomas displayed with other treasures.

to create a tight brief—all decisions need to be based on your vision, your requirements, and your pocket.

I bring in kitchen planners on every job because the kitchen is the most complex of rooms and possibly the most important, since it is where most of us spend the majority of our time. Achieving a workable open-plan space with three or four zones demands a meticulous and organized approach. At the first meeting, show the planner your mood board of ideas displaying the elements and furniture you wish to be worked into the scheme; explain your brief with as much detail as possible to get to the core of the design and the range of options. How many zones can you accommodate in your space? How will each one be lit? Do you want

air conditioning or surround sound? Will you need to install a suspended ceiling for extraction and ducting? What combination of surface materials will work in terms of both practicality and look? What proportion of your budget have you set aside for this room? Kitchen planners will have answers and solutions, but first you need to make the call on each question. Let the ideas flow and investigate your options, but stick to your brief to keep the kitchen workable for you, and compromise with care where you have to.

Even though most specialist kitchen companies term their designs universal, this is not always the case. The same concept will not necessarily work for a couple with children as for a divorced man. Gender

does come into it—boys like toys, and men tend to want it "easy" in the cooking and eating areas, with perhaps the emphasis on the chill-out-and-play zone. A design's conception will always depend on your circumstances and how you like to live.

## Surfaces and finishes

There are wonderful surfaces to play with in kitchens—generally wood, lacquer, glass, stone, stainless steel, and ceramic. Whatever you choose has to work for where you are putting it. I have successfully had wooden floors in kitchens (they need periodic refinishing) and less successfully had concrete and resin (they can crack if the substratum is not solid).

Think of the tones of color and the varying textures of the materials you like while also thinking practically because you want to make connections between the zones to give the room its balance.

## Design solutions: My kitchen

The layout of my kitchen takes up the majority of the first floor. There is an island-bar chill-out zone at the front of the house, which flows into the working zone, which flows into the dining zone at the back, which opens into the garden. I knew from the outset that I wanted a comfortable and open series of spaces in a monochromatic, textural palette. I wanted a fireplace in the kitchen, up on the wall like a painting.

**MY KITCHEN** (*above*) was custom-made by Boffi in this mocha-toned lacquer finish. The cupboards have a slim banner-style sliding door that allows me to see and access my dinnerware easily. I always wanted a fireplace in my kitchen, and this BD Design fire sculpture has been set in a custom-made fireplace with a chrome edge, mounted on the wall like a painting. The chrome and leather bar chairs were custom-made by Talisman, based on one of their original pieces.

My look is a tidy mess, and I like being able to pull things from the shelves without opening a door. This led to a new design of sliding cupboard-front panels in place of doors, which read to the eye as charismatic vertical banners because they do not span the entire width of the cupboard shelves. Boffi built the kitchen units in a special mocha-toned lacquer, and the feeling in the space is that of a furnished room, rather than a wall-to-wall storage area. The use of milk glass (toughened glass with a painted and foil back) gave me a superb working surface for all the countertops. It is very tough and practical, as well as beautiful and reflective. I use it in place of stone and wood surfaces all over the house because it is price-savvy and relatively easy to install. These are personal examples illustrating how I reached certain design solutions and will perhaps inspire some original and practical solutions for your own project.

## Kitchen lighting

Getting the lighting right is enormously important, but it does not need to be overly complex. All lighting should be controllable, by individual dimmer switches or a main preset control panel for each zone, which can be programmed for instant lighting settings. The principle is to have task lights by which to prepare food and ambient light to create and enhance mood. Discreet under-cupboard lighting is a must, and it is worth considering top-lighting the cupboards to add a soft glow. I chose surface-mounted, globe-shaped nickel lights, having tired of the pockmarked look created by recessed ceiling lights. I like to see lights,

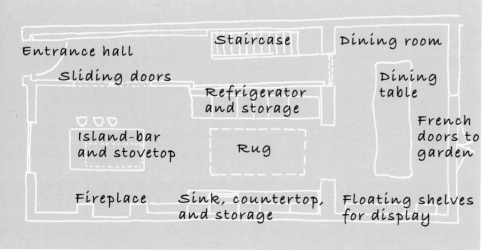

Entrance hall
Sliding doors
Staircase
Dining room
Dining table
Refrigerator and storage
Island-bar and stovetop
Rug
French doors to garden
Fireplace
Sink, countertop, and storage
Floating shelves for display

and I also love to see the detail of a nickel screw in a fixing plate—it adds to the overall beauty of the many layers of interest and texture.

## Appliances and furnishings

For some, the choice of appliances alludes to the level their cooking has reached; for others, it is purely the joy of having the latest must-have items. I have a thing about Sub-Zero refrigerators (the Aston Martin of refrigerators, freezers, and wine coolers), am very particular about faucets (pieces of sculpture), would never be without a faucet that provides instant boiling water, and like gas stovetops that run in a line of up to five rings (they are practical and look incredible). I install air conditioning and like downdraft range hoods that pop up from the countertop.

Whatever your design, never underestimate the value of comfort in a room where you spend so much time. Instead of stools for my island-bar, I had some retro leather and chrome chairs altered to the correct height (and additional ones made). Everyone loves this part of my kitchen; it is not only the chill-and-chat zone, it is a place to work, read, breakfast, and generally "be."

**TWO VIEWS** of my kitchen (*above and opposite top*) show how the working and dining areas relate. I wanted the dining area to have its own character, while still being part of the space. I drew the outline of the oak table with a free hand, so that it would feel like a farmhouse table in a contemporary setting. The Christian Liaigre Velin chairs have been mixed with equally comfortable leather benches for a look that is smart, modern, and informal. The Boffi cabinetry has a beautifully reflective polished-lacquer finish. Practical milk-glass counters and backsplashes keep the look simple.

**THE CUPBOARD FRONTS** (*right*) were made as sliding banners that do not fully enclose the storage space because I like dinnerware to be on view.

# KEYNOTES FOR A SUCCESSFUL KITCHEN

**The kitchen is an all-embracing center for family life, where spaces are opened up, one into the other, for preparing and cooking food, eating, chatting, working, and playing, as we all enjoy a more communal lifestyle.**

Locate your kitchen in the right place within your home, based on how you like to live and on the space available to you, even if this means resiting it. This is most easily achieved by going through your checklist of questions and answers, in order to determine how many zones you require within your given space and the optimum layout for each. Choices of materials, finishes, lighting, appliances, and furnishings, and whether or not to have surround sound and air conditioning, are all decisions you should make on the basis of good research at specialist kitchen companies, prior to hiring the kitchen-design company that appeals both to your instinct and to your budget. Thorough planning is the key to a successful kitchen and will save you thousands of dollars.

**WORK SPACE** in a kitchen should be determined by how much of a cook you are, and your kitchen designers will help you to achieve the best possible layout for your space. Choose appliances such as ovens and refrigerators to suit your cooking skills, as well as for their looks.

**GLAMOUR** is introduced through your choice of materials—glass, wood, and marble make a classic Kelly Hoppen combination— and appliances, which add to the impact. Your faucets are pieces of sculpture, as are the stools and chairs.

**DINING** in the kitchen is the norm, so integrate a dining area into the scheme so that there is a seamless flow of materials from one space to the next,

especially in your choice of flooring. A fireplace set high on the wall is a strong modern feature that reads like art and adds soul to the space.

**FLOORING MATERIALS** such as wood, stone, and poured resin or concrete are all well-used and practical choices. Make sure that they are finished correctly, so that they are durable and do not stain.

**PRACTICALITIES** such as air conditioning and extraction should be specified by a professional kitchen designer and may require a ceiling cavity for ducting.

**LIGHTING** should be flexible and controllable, to allow for different moods and activities. Ensure that there is sufficient task lighting in the working part of the kitchen.

**ISLAND-BARS** on double-sided central units can be the cooking zone, as well as a place to eat, chat, and work. They are a great way of maximizing the use of available space.

**FURNISH** the kitchen as you would any other room, with comfortable, chic seating and well-planned lighting.

**THIS URBAN KITCHEN** (*above and left*) is as pleasing by day as it is by night, as a result of the versatile lighting scheme by Robert Clift Lighting— a preset control means that light levels can be switched to suit different moods. The predominantly white scheme is grounded by dark wood floors and lifted by the repetition of nickel in the Mirage stools by Danetti, the client's own chairs, and the custom-made fireplace surround. The glass island top is in fine contrast with the white marble table— a simple design based on a console table. The glass pendant lights were incorporated into the design at the outset. Shades filter the daylight and keep the look sharp.

# KELLY'S *TOP PICKS*

LOW-LEVEL, LOW-GLOW LIGHTING that makes units appear to float above gently lit floors

FIREPLACES set high into the wall as easily seen "art," to introduce a focal point as well as comfort and warmth

REFLECTIVE SURFACES for the glamour and balance that they bring to the space

ISLAND-BARS on central units, which maximize the use of space in a kitchen and provide a practical seating area that will be used more often than you imagine

TEXTURE AND CONTRAST in the form of matte
and shine—the cream leather stools with metal edging
in play with the milk-glass counter are perfection

# DINING

FOR MOST OF US, DINING IS ONE OF LIFE'S CHERISHED RITUALS. IT IS WHEN YOU EAT, TALK, AND SHARE, AND COME TOGETHER FOR THE HIGH DAYS AND HOLIDAYS OF LIFE.

*Few of us have separate dining rooms*—the room in the house that was once dedicated to formal dining may have become a study or private retreat, or have been integrated into a large cooking-eating-living zone. Many people create an informal yet smart and modern dining zone within the kitchen. Any dining space, whether created as a zone or set in its own dedicated room, must suit how you live and with whom you live. The dining room forms its own bedrock to family and social life, and can be one of those places you do not want to leave because the atmosphere is charged with good feelings.

## Siting the dining area

Dining rooms can be designed as successfully within great halls, where collections, paintings, or sculptures are showcased, as they can be set within a semiscreened area of a living room. Think of all the

**TAKING A DESIGN FROM CONCEPT TO REALITY** begins with the client's requirements and my vision. The CAD illustration (*below*) showed the client the design, rendered with almost photographic clarity. In the finished dining room (*right*), the client's artwork—*Topsy Turvy* by Daniel Kelly—has replaced the proposed shelving, but otherwise the design is true to the vision. Christian Liaigre's Velin chairs and lacquered Continent sideboard are graceful in the space, which also holds a grand piano.

*The dining zone is your stage ... so when you are designing, feel free to play with your fantasies and sense of light-heartedness.*

**THE MOOD IN THIS DINING ZONE** (*above*) is light and modern because of the monochromatic mix of charcoal, black, and white with warm-toned wood floors and antique books on the floating shelves. Textural balance is achieved by the open-weave Non-Random Lights by Bertjan Pot, wavy-edged oak table, faux-leather upholstered benches, and La Fibule Bridge chairs. I designed the shutters and the fireplace surround, which is placed high on the wall as though a piece of art.

exciting, beautiful places you have been, and pull some of those elements into your design—the way a table is screened to create intimacy, the surprising combination of scrubbed wood and Plexiglass, the showy quality of a cocktail bar with banks of bottles and rows of glassware. Eating in a dining zone characterized by glamorous upholstery at the center of a glass-and-steel kitchen can be as enjoyable an experience as a grand banquet in a room that houses an extraordinary wall installation of organic forms. The dining zone is your stage for all-the-time eating and lots-of-time lunches, evening meals, and full-scale dinner parties, so when you are designing, feel free to play with your fantasies and sense of light-heartedness.

The majority of the people for whom I design do not have separate dining rooms because they prefer integrated dining room–kitchens or dining-living rooms. In all of these spaces, however, I maximize the versatility of the design, so that each could be set up for all sorts of dining and, in some cases, other uses. A table in a kitchen zone is never just for eating because it is truly the main gathering point of the room. I always advise my clients to make the most of every inch of space in their home. This is of particular value in urban apartments, where the allocated kitchen space is often no more than a galley from which the dining area has to extend, sometimes into the hall.

## The layout

I often state that there are no rules in design, just invaluable guidelines that you can use as a framework to your specific brief. The first step is to assess your space in terms of the grid, to get the lines of the room in balance (see page 63), then figure out the maximum size of the table and the amount of space that will be taken up by the surrounding chairs. You need to make sure that you will be able to move around and behind the chairs when people are seated at the table, in order to serve food with ease. At this stage, you should also work out your storage, whether it is a freestanding sideboard, a combination of cupboards and shelves for display, or an entire wall dedicated to a china and glass store hidden behind sliding-panel doors.

## Lighting and music

Address the existing lighting scheme and decide on any new elements. Lighting is your chief source to set the mood and will give even the humblest of spaces its own sparkle. A classic treatment is a chandelier hung low over the table with even lower-level wall lights casting light and shadow to the floor and bouncing it up to the ceiling, uplighting the space in a flattering manner. In place of a single central light, there can be a series of modern glass bubbles that

cluster over the length of the table, to give an overall wide-reaching glow. A dining room lit exclusively by wall lights that wrap around the space can be very dramatic, almost medieval, in reference. Dimmers are essential in a dining area, and the lighting scheme should always include candlelight.

I wire for music throughout the house and advise that you do the same, especially if you are doing any new wiring—this is the point when it is most practical to add a good sound system, if your budget allows. Stand-alone sound systems and iPod docks with correctly sited speakers are also options.

## Furnishings and table dressings

The centerpiece of any dining space must be the table and chairs. It is their charisma that will set the tone of the room and give it its identity. I rarely specify

**THE DESIGN CONCEPT** here was to create a delightfully unexpected dining space within a kitchen that opened through folding doors into the living space beyond. Furnished with such an eclectic mix of styles and textures, the dining zone feels like a dedicated room, rather than a zone within an open-plan space. Texture is crucial in all of my work, and here the acrylic dining chairs make a beautiful play against the solidity of the white-painted oak table by St. Paul Home and the strong lines of Kevin Reilly's Altar light.

**A TRIUMPH OF TEXTURE** (opposite) reigns in this chalet dining room, where taupe-toned wood, horn, metal, and linen combine for a feeling of luxurious warmth. The furnishings are grandly informal—horn Eclipse chandeliers from Ochre hang above the Contemporanea table that is surrounded by dining chairs from B&B Italia, with slipcovers to keep the mood light. The deep, thick-looped carpet grounds the dining zone.

**AN ECLECTIC MIX** (below top) creates wow factor when it is handled well. The white decor, with a plaster wall runner, and black floor and woodwork enhance the sense of space, while the quirky wood chairs and white-glass chandeliers—both from Asiatides—and the custom-made wooden table create interest and drama. The furniture is arranged on a leather-bordered silk rug, leaving plenty of space around it.

**ALL THE ELEMENTS** (below bottom) in this custom-made dining room in the main hallway of the house balance one another, while still being interesting and inviting. I designed the chairs, upholstered with embossed leather from Alma, to go with the Gosling table inlaid with mother-of-pearl (below right). The Ring Screens are an essential part of the balance; they demarcate the dining space and create a sense of intimacy.

matching tables and chairs because I am drawn to contrast and balance—the masculine and the feminine, the bold and the subtle, the old and the new. This approach gives you enormous freedom in putting together the table, chairs, and benches. A vintage pine table can work with iconic butterfly chairs; a glass- or zinc-topped table mixes well with contemporary upholstered benches; and a white lacquered oak table surrounded by vintage Plexiglass chairs will have enormous power and appeal in an otherwise modern space, just as a metal table teamed with satin damask will surprise and please the eye. How you execute the dressing up and dressing down of the table will overlay the room with its formal or informal edge. All of these examples can be dressed to suit breakfast, coffee, lunch, supper, tea, cocktails, and dinner. Each can also function as a part-time base station for phone calls, bills, homework, and e-mails, as and when necessary, so that you really utilize your space.

A trestle table dressed with a mix of vintage linens and china is as much of a statement as a table inlaid with marquetry and set with silverware and crystal. Your creative armory contains infinite possibilities in terms of linens, runners, napkins and napkin rings, china, glassware, tin, silverware, flatware, crystal, tealights, candles, candlesticks, lacquer, flowers, vases, coral, rope, and pebbles. Keep the story on your table edited to three or four textural elements in a tonal range of color, so it is cohesive and strong. The flowers and the food will add more than enough color and accent.

# KEYNOTES FOR A SUCCESSFUL DINING AREA

**Smart and modern dining zones, whether integrated into open-plan living spaces or more formally set within a dedicated room, should be designed for mood and theater, as dining is one of life's best rituals.**

Use your imagination, and draw upon memories of places where you have dined to inspire the design of your dining space. The way a table is screened in a restaurant can translate to your own open-plan space, or the sheer grandeur of a historic mansion might spark an idea for a series of low chandeliers over the dining table and a collection of fabulous glassware. Use the grid to help you get the lines of the room in play and the flow of space balanced. Lighting is of prime importance and must be controllable because this will give even the humblest of dining spaces its own sense of magic.

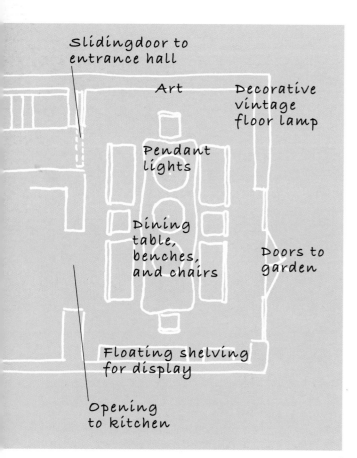

Slidingdoor to entrance hall

Art

Decorative vintage floor lamp

Pendant lights

Dining table, benches, and chairs

Doors to garden

Floating shelving for display

Opening to kitchen

**THE TABLE** is never just for eating; it is the main gathering point of the room. This solid oak farmhouse-style table (*opposite, top right*), with its freestyle hand-drawn organic edge, has even more personality because it is unexpectedly set within a contemporary dining zone.

**COMFORT** is crucial because you will spend so much time sitting at the table. Upholstered seating can be provided in a mix of benches and chairs, as I have done in my own home. I rarely use matching tables and chairs—I like a spirited contrast in texture.

**DISPLAY** is such fun in a dining room. The tabletop itself can be finished with a series of repeated objects, candles, flowers, or plants—in this case,

tiny bonsai trees, planted by John Carter in long, slim Plexiglass troughs made for me by Rob Van Helden (*opposite, top left*) or posies of the palest pink nude roses in organic ceramic vessels by Absolute Flowers (*opposite, top right*). Shelving is an excellent display medium, where delightful and eclectic objects, pictures, and books can be put on show and changed around as the mood takes you. Floating shelves are elegant and do not dominate the space.

**ART** allows you to express your personality and the dining room is a perfect space to display a favorite sculpture, photograph, or painting. This work by Peter Beard (*opposite, top left*) makes a stunning focal point on the wall at one end of my dining table.

**LIGHTING** is extremely flattering when diffused and set low over a dining table. A repeated series of identical shades is extremely effective and, when seen from a distance, these large circular shades sit beautifully within the overall architecture of the open-plan space. Additional ceiling lights can be like my preferred surface-mounted vintage spots, which are directed toward the walls for a soft wall-wash effect—never directed overhead because you want the most flattering light possible. In addition, sculptural floor lamps, such as my vintage metal leaf-shaped lamp (*opposite, top left*), add a decorative element, while candles are a must at night. Lighting must always be controlled on several circuits, by dimmer switches or a preset control panel.

# KELLY'S *TOP PICKS*

ORGANICALLY SHAPED sheer light shades that are repeated in a trio over a curved-edged oak table

QUIRKY ELEMENTS, such as this vintage metal leaf floor lamp, found at a flea market, and table accessories that are fresh and surprising within the context of the space

THE THEATER OF DINING—fluid crystal chandeliers and individually painted chairs create the show at Gary Rhodes's London restaurant.

TEXTURAL CONTRAST between the table and chairs, so they do not match, but sit in harmony with one another

DESIGN WIT that pushes the
boundaries and makes for a genuinely
eclectic combination—here it is horn,
wood, metal, and linen

**GRACEFUL LIVING** in this large open space is kept intimate by the placement of furniture in three zones— a seating area designed for socializing in the foreground, a more cozy area for relaxing in front of the fire and a reading area at the other end of the room (see page 149). Here the Wanda leather and linen sofas and suede armchairs by Promemoria, with my signature pillows, are arranged on a large silk rug that defines the zone. I designed the hanging ball light to drop down over the sculptural wood coffee table by Jerome Abel Seguin. At night, the Modenature Move floor lamp casts a welcoming pool of light over the pair of armchairs. A focal point of the seating area is the sculpture by Richard Hoey on the curved plaster wall by Polidori Barbera.

# LIVING ROOMS

LIVING ROOMS CAN BE INTEGRATED INTO AN OPEN-PLAN DESIGN JUST AS EFFECTIVELY AS THEY CAN BE SEPARATELY GRAND. THEY CAN BE APPOINTED AS A SERIES OF PLACES TO SIT, READ, AND RELAX, AND BE AS RIGHT FOR A PARTY AS FOR NIGHTS IN WITH FRIENDS.

*Think hard about the role of your living space in your home before you start planning the design.*

Is it going to be an informal family room that is part work, part rest, and part play, or will it be a formal drawing room styled for display and collections? Always begin with you, your vision, and your needs.

Study the "bones" of the room, its very structure, and use the grid to help you to see the room three-dimensionally (see page 63). The grid, zoning, and flow bring each and every room together. Any architectural features are to be respected, particularly in a period property, but all too often you will be dealing with the mistakes and cover-ups of others, and you often have to strip down a room to its barest bones, in order to layer it back up again. Original features should be integrated into your design. Crown molding, for example, is an excellent feature for a contemporary interior—it acts like a timeline in the house, declaring age or provenance. In the absence of notable features, look for means of introducing them. A successful way to do this is to create openings and replace doors, often taking them to full height. A fireplace—so welcoming in a space—is another obvious feature that can be left as it is, improved, replaced, or installed. The architectural elements create the basic grace and proportions of a space. Your job is to emphasize and harmonize, and often to compromise.

## Creating your scheme

Work with the grid, so that you can see all the lines of the room, and keep them in mind when you are thinking through the design. Where are the windows and how do they relate to the fireplace, the doors, and other features? This gives you the beginnings of a layout.

**THE LIVELY TEXTURAL CONTRAST** (*above left*) of the wood, glass, suede, silk, and linen makes this seating zone luxurious and welcoming.

**FLOATING SHELVES** (*opposite top*) in the fireplace alcoves draw the eye to the end of the room, where a pair of Promemoria Wanda sofas face each other over an arrangement of Christian Liaigre Flibuste tables. The Porta Romana floor lamps underline the symmetry.

**ALMOST PERFECT SYMMETRY** (right) is also in play at the other end of the living room, which is dominated by the custom black-stained bookcase that takes up most of the wall. Promemoria chaises have been upholstered with rich chocolate suede from Holly Hunt. The Inthai faux snakeskin on the divan adds to the subtlety of texture, as do the silk rug, bronze floor lamps from Porta Romana, and wood Spider's Nest tables from Tucker Robbins.

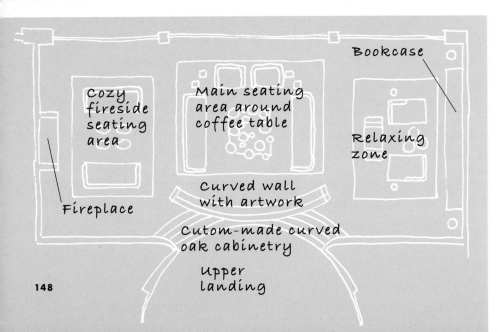

Bookcase

Cozy fireside seating area

Main seating area around coffee table

Relaxing zone

Fireplace

Curved wall with artwork

Cutom-made curved oak cabinetry

Upper landing

Think about where the main seating will be; what the view into another part of the room and beyond into the garden, kitchen, or other area will be; how many seating zones you need; where the television will be; and so on. Answering these questions will help you to decide on a layout and define how you will move through and around the zones or the space as a whole. At this stage, I hold another image in my mind of corsetry, good old-fashioned boning with stays, which

you tighten to create a perfect body. I relate this to the room via my grid, and I like the sexiness of this concept.

By the time I choose the floor, I already have a picture in my mind of what all the other materials will be—the fabrics, furniture, lighting, cabinetry, and wall finishes are all laid out on my mood boards. Flooring must be timeless, and not a fashion statement because it will be down for a long time and is beyond expensive to change. I have to know the fabrics and

the textures of every other aspect of the room, sometimes including the art, so that when I choose the floor I know what additional texture or tone to introduce, whether to create a contrasting flooring banner by mixing wood and stone or whether the room needs darkly stained oak with bordered silk carpets. I know that my grid lines are creating the right proportion and drama, the symmetry or asymmetry, and that the lines and texture of the

**THE FLOATING CHIMNEY** is the central feature in this chalet, and the furniture has been arranged in the spaces on either side, for chilling out and watching television, sitting by the fire, and dining. The color palette is classic Kelly Hoppen, where taupe, white, silver, and chocolate have high notes of orange and subtle purple. I love the specialist plaster finish on the chimney, together with the textural mix of the statement Mule Deer Cascade chandeliers by Antler Art, the horn Eclipse pendants from Ochre, the Novasuede used to upholster the Promemoria Madame A armchairs, the hide ottoman from Minotti, and the steel log basket by David Turner.

flooring are pulling the whole together, to ground the room. That way, I know that the visual play will be harmonious between all the ingredients in the room.

A few of my clients have wanted one-space wonders that combine living space, home movie theater, dining area, study, and bar. Others want gracefully laid-out rooms with two or three seating zones, the principal one being centered around the fireplace. A living room can work with an original, exotic, or quirky coffee table at its center, with groups of chairs and sofas surrounding it, leaving virtually no furniture at the walls and therefore clear space for shelving displays or art. For some, a spectacular living space is a sofa in the middle of the room, an exquisite light, and a single piece of astonishing art on the wall. Living rooms can be split in two, to define a live-relax space and a live-work space. For me, a living room must have a sexy, easy glamour and be suitable for relaxing, as well as for entertaining and being with my girlfriends. What defines any well-designed living space, whether formal or informal, is that, however many zones are being created or however many different functions you are packing into the space, each part of the room has its own identity while still retaining the feeling that it flows freely into the next.

There are, of course, the practicalities to consider. Your mood boards, sketches, and architect's plans (and/ or your own) are your base-point tools and triggers. The grid has given you a framework for getting the space together. Your vision has defined the personality,

**A SINGLE SOFA** (*top left*) that I designed sits well with the quirky black iron side table from Monpas on the leather-bordered silk rug. The white console table from Megaron provides a surface for display and grounds the pictures above it.

**A SIMPLE ARRANGEMENT** (*center left*) of a Belmondo modular sofa and ottoman from Meridiani and a Piccolo armchair by Holly Hunt around a coffee table is anchored by the leather-edged rug and emphasizes the lines of the room. The photography is from the Michael Hoppen Gallery.

**THE STAR PIECE** (*bottom left*) in my living room is a fabulous, vintage, polished steel and brass coffee table. Its shape has a dynamic quality and works well with the clean-lined Modenature Chelsea sofa covered in damask linen.

**RED IS A PERFECT ACCENT** (*opposite*) in this living space that leads into a dining room, where the Christian Liaigre Augustin sofa, Gallet ottoman, L.N.A. cocktail table, and Chantecaille floor lamps have been put together with Dennis Miller's red Gobbi Club chairs and a metal Oval table by Robert Kuo.

function, and flow of the room. Now spend time in the room with your sketchpad, tape measure, masking tape, and chalk. Draw out the furniture using chalk, and mask off items for the walls, including any paneling, mirrors, and artwork. Mark up the position and sizes of the wall lights. Take a virtual tour through the space in your mind, then take an actual one, to make sure that there is sufficient room between the coffee table and the sofa, between the table and the door. This is the literal flow of space and will prevent you from designing a room that feels too full or awkward. Take large samples of fabrics to see how they look and "hang" in the space. Leave the mood boards leaning against the walls, so that you can refer to them again and again. These are all things that I do to get design right.

## Lighting and mood

Pay attention to the lighting (see pages 88–99). A well-lit room will always have its own wow and welcome factor, however modest its features or decoration, but a room where the lighting has not received due care

will never sing out, whatever the decoration. The more you can vary and control the lighting the better, and I strongly suggest that you hire a lighting consultant, to achieve an overall brilliant result. A critical piece of underwear to a room's outerwear, lighting gives its own kind of structure, spirit, and energy.

My final thoughts on living rooms are about looks and feelings—the feeling of a home is what people remember. I spend a great deal of time and energy on balance and flow. I instinctively use feng shui, whereby the energy in the space is harmonious, fortuitous, and working for you. I naturally create a mix of old and new, soft and hard (or yin and yang), and always work texture to the nth at every level. The furniture I choose has presence and panache. My homes have always had a eclectic element—vintage, contemporary, ultramodern, antique, and so on—because I mix it all up, but that does not mean any old mix will do. Eclectic means choosing one or two pieces that have nothing to do with anything else in the room. Eclectic is a point that draws the eye.

**THE RELAXING ZONE** in this home is off the circular landing and has curved sliding doors. You can see how the CAD drawing (*opposite, bottom left*) relates to the actual design. The wall unit is custom-made, and the furniture includes a generous-sized L-shaped sofa and ottoman from Flexform, Bishop ceramic side tables from India Mahdavi, and an inviting leather easy chair from De Sede. The seating is all perfectly placed for relaxing in comfort in front of the large television, and the leather chair both reclines and swivels—to either watch television or have a conversation with people on the sofa. The giant floor lamps from Meridiani add a certain theatricality to the space.

# KEYNOTES FOR A SUCCESSFUL LIVING ROOM

**A living room integrated into an open multipurpose space can be just as successful as a separate, more formal room. Ultimately, what you choose will depend on the size and layout of your home and your preference, but in either case the design must reflect both your vision and your needs.**

Use the grid, zoning, and flow principles to bring the design together and find the right balance between the architecture of the house and your ideals. Retain original features as a general rule because period elements are more than comfortable in contemporary interiors. In homes with no character, doors can be restructured to run full height—a dramatic and space-enhancing treatment. Design the entire room, from the windows to the soft furnishings, before deciding on the flooring. That way, you will know the character of every decorative element before committing to the final layer of tone and texture that will unite the whole. Hire a lighting specialist to ensure that the living space is adaptable to different uses and moods.

Television · Natural light · Drapes · Artificial Light · Art · Glamour · Flooring

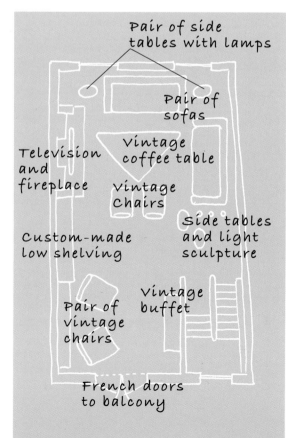

Pair of side tables with lamps

Pair of sofas

Television and fireplace

Vintage coffee table

Vintage Chairs

Custom-made low shelving

Side tables and light sculpture

Pair of vintage chairs

Vintage buffet

French doors to balcony

**GLAMOUR** is the chief ingredient in my own living space, where a monochromatic palette has created a serene vision of photographic perfection, fulfilling my aim to make my living room seem like a stunning black-and-white picture. I have chosen everything from materials to furniture and accessories with this in mind, and pieces such as the Flibuste table (*left*) by Christian Liaigre are key.

**FLOORING** is ebony-stained original boards, which give the space an air of integrity; they are in perfect balance with all the other black elements, from the side tables to the wall unit, because there is a change of textural pace between each.

**NATURAL LIGHT** fills a room with magical ever-changing light and reflection. Make the most of it with sheer drapes, which softly filter the light while providing privacy.

**ARTIFICIAL LIGHT** has been harnessed to give a low, soft glow at floor level, and nickel surface-mounted directional ceiling lights have been chosen in favor of downlighters. The combination of the two creates the most flattering light.

**ART** is such an essential and personal ingredient. I love photography and especially love images of glamorous women, such as *Jessica in Lace Dress* by Louise Bobbe, from Stephanie Hoppen Gallery.

**TELEVISIONS** on show are a signature of mine. Here the chimney breast has been clad with a giant panel of glossy black glass, into which the screen is set. The effect is beautiful.

**DRAPES** can be changed according to your mood or the seasons. The view of my living space (*above*) shows what a remarkable effect a slim banner detail can have on sheer drapes when compared to a plain set (*right*). This banner is made from a strip of black carpet tape sewn onto plain white voile. I love simple iron curtain poles because they are understated and elegant, and do not detract from the fabric or overpower the room.

## DISPLAY KEYNOTES

Change displays around every few months to refresh the look and feeling of your home.

Use the impact of repetition—with pieces of furniture, as well as objects.

Work within a color code so that your displays are connected to the room's design.

**THE REPETITION** (*left*) of three glossy black lacquer Christian Liaigre Flibuste tables is striking, especially with the scale of the tiny glass-encased moss balls.

**A GLORIOUS COMBINATION** (*opposite, top left*) against a backdrop of black-and-white photography is as simple as a vintage bronze lizard sculpture on a bronze Ajoure side table by Christian Liaigre.

**WARM TAUPE TONES** (*opposite, top right*) are always harmonious and mix well with like-toned elements, such as these pewter bowls, dark-stained wood Promemoria Mose table, and bronze Porta Romana lamp.

**CUSTOM-MADE FLOATING SHELVES** (*opposite, bottom left*) give you surfaces on which to display objects and photographs, which here includes a portrait of Brigitte Bardot by Terry O'Neill.

**WHITE CERAMIC BOTTLES** (*opposite, bottom right*) make a powerful display on a blackened oak floor.

**THE ECLECTIC COMBINATIONS** (*opposite*) of both shape and materials—the finely crafted metal frame, glazed-linen upholstery, and velvet scatter pillow with contrasting band—make this elegant armchair by Ego Zeroventiquattro one of the star items in this living space. The glazed linen was chosen to tone with the leather-trimmed silk rug.

**INTRICATELY EMBOSSED LEATHER** (*left*) from Alma has been used to upholster these comfortable padded dining chairs, which I designed to work with the custom-made Gosling table. The cream color and swirling pattern of the leather perfectly complement the table's mother-of-pearl inlay.

# FURNISHINGS AND UPHOLSTERY

**Upholstery is utterly transformational. It is an exciting element of any project— a kind of art in its own right—and should never be underestimated.**

Upholstery can turn the mediocre into a masterpiece and overlay inherited junk and other pieces with irreverent wit or radical chic. It can be a brilliant way of introducing an accent color or element of surprise into a scheme.

I have an obvious passion for the subject, for upholstery is where you have artistic license to expand upon the three-dimensionality of a room. It is a whole new playground for textural contrasts that appeal to the touch and increase visual delight. In upholstery, you are adding more layers of comfort, interest, luxury, depth, and character.

## Choosing fabrics

You can upholster in fabrics from fine linens to basic scrims, in an immense choice of silk, satin, velvet, chenille, mohair, tweed, wool, cashmere, felt, plastics, leather, and hide. Fabrics that are shredded, pleated, or twisted can also come into your upholstery portfolio—some may even be splattered with paints, strewn with graffiti, embossed, or delicately decorated with silver leaf or gilt work. Have fun searching for interesting materials. You will be surprised by how inspiring such lively textural combinations can be and what they can do to the punch and pitch of a room.

I always start with a linen for any scheme and build from there because a design without linen just does not feel right. It is a good idea to do an individual upholstery mood board for each room because you can pin on photographs of the chairs, sofas, ottomans, and stools alongside the fabrics. Put images of trims, hides, upholstery tacks, buttons, and stitch styles onto the board as well, to see how they work with your colors, tones, and textures; this will help to keep you on track and moving toward making your ideas real.

I do not have preconceived notions as to what fabric will be put on this piece or that item. I keep the process open until I know how I want to pace and balance the room, and I do this by putting the fabrics together into stories until I find a combination that is fresh and appropriate to the space. Often, a room can start with a star item—perhaps a vintage chair that is perfect as it is, or another that has great bone structure and simply needs to be redressed—and the rest of the design detail flows from that decision.

I always work to build texture and contrast, whether I am designing rock-n-roll style with embossed leather and velour, or having an Audrey Hepburn moment of luscious red silk velvet. Sheers that shimmer look all the more delicate against rough tweed or wool. Metallic stitching stands out on felts. Suede, satin, cashmere, and wool is always timelessly and quietly luxurious in textural combination.

*Upholstery is a whole new playground for textural contrasts that play to the touch and increase visual delight.*

LINEN—an essential, practical, and versatile fabric and the starting point of any scheme. It combines brilliantly with velvet, satin, and faded damask.

TEXTURAL COMBINATIONS that give the room "punch," while still being elegant and luxurious

SIMPLE DETAILS that give a chic finish to a piece

You must consider what the item of furniture is going to be used for because this will define its covering. Is your bedroom chair for reading or is it a clotheshorse in disguise? Do you like to sink into your sofa with feather-and-down-filled pillows or sit more upright and supported? These choices are as personal as the pillow and mattress you choose to sleep upon, so ultimately comfort is a chief consideration. Be smart in your choices: parachute silk will last for ten minutes on a chair, whereas an upholstery-grade silk will wear for years. If you are in doubt about the practicality of a fabric for how you want to use it, check with your upholsterer.

## Design details

I like sofas that have a skirt that grows from the main seat cushion because this look is endlessly modern. I like the tension created in soft furnishings by the combination of a faded damask and a linen, a satin and a linen, a velvet and a linen—this could be on the sofa between the base and the cushions, or on the front and back of a dining chair. Where there are button details, how do you want the buttons? Do you want buttoning at all? I am enchanted by the simplicity of an upholsterer's X-shaped stitch, which is the traditional way to mark a button's position, and I use this as a finished detail rather than having the button stitched on at all. I seek the

**RED PLAYS A VITAL ROLE** (*opposite, top left and right*) in this beautifully balanced neutral scheme, with its mix of taupe tones and textures. Christian Liaigre's off-white linen Augustin sofa and taupe leather Autan chaise are grounded on a ribbed silk carpet around the L.N.A. cocktail table. The warmth of tone is enriched by the red leather Gallet ottoman and the red glazed-linen pillows—the addition of a horn button is perfect in relation to the taupe tones. I like to lift a design with vintage items, such as the metal lamp on the Robert Kuo Oval table, and contemporary pieces, such as the white bowls, also by Robert Kuo.

**THE RED MATTE SUEDE** (*opposite, bottom left*) of the Gobbi Club chairs by Dennis Miller dominates a second seating zone within the same living space. Together with a Chantecaille floor lamp and Flibuste table by Christian Liaigre, they are anchored on a silk rug with red leather edging.

**THE SOFT TAUPE LEATHER UPHOLSTERY** (*opposite, bottom right*) on my Hostess chair has chic flat seams instead of piping. It plays against the delicate open-weave drapes, together with the Robert Kuo O table and a cast-bronze Ochre lamp.

**THE SOFT GRAY SILK VELVET** from Manuel Canovas on the inviting Martini double armchair and the Minotti ottoman is in perfect contrast with the wood-lined walls and sheer drapes in this chalet. The orange velvet pillow adds a burst of color and warmth.

simplicity in all details. I like to reveal a kind of pure nakedness, where I strip an item to the raw, rather than unnecessarily covering it up. This has parallels with fashion, when women sometimes wear underwear as outerwear. I like to think of some elements of upholstery emerging in the same way.

The way you put together your fabrics for the soft furnishings in a room can be formatted to give you the crispness of a tailored suit, with leather, linen, and velvet, or it can be softly chic without being shabby, by the same linen weave being repeated in many different natural tones and soft colors throughout the room. A chair that is finished in woven horsehair will have an inherent sharp quality, while another that is covered in buttery suede will read as being sensuously soft. One that is covered with embossed mock-croc will evoke Gatsby-esque, almost vulgar glamour. If you are in Garbo mode, satin and sheers, and fur and kid, will set the tone. Lace is rock-star sexy, especially with velour, mohair, and raw silk, as is a chair finished with a curtain of minuscule beads revealing glimpses of its nicely turned legs. This is what I mean about artistic license—you have the freedom to experiment, to evoke, and to create, and ultimately to pile your personality into the room.

**THE SIZE AND TEXTURE** (*above right*) of the pillows on this Meridiani sofa make a bold statement. The metallic glazed-linen and velvet fabrics by Holly Hunt are offset beautifully by the large pearl buttons.

**TWO DIFFERENT FABRICS** (*below right*) can be used to great effect. This built-in banquette is to my design, upholstered in damask with cross-stitch detailing instead of buttons, with cushions in silk velvet.

## FANTASTIC FURNISHING

- New upholstery is a brilliant way to give your furniture a face-lift and bring radical chic to inherited pieces or items bought at flea markets.

- It is advisable to create specific furnishings mood boards for each room, onto which you can pin fabric choices, trims, and buttons alongside pictures of the items to be reupholstered.

- Build up your fabric story to add more layers of comfort, interest, luxury, and character to a room through textural and tonal combinations.

# signature
## KELLY'S
## DETAILS
## PILLOWS

Pillows have long been a signature element of any room I have designed. Far more than a finishing touch, pillows embody the textural quality and comfort in the room as a whole; they reflect and complement all the other elements within it. A simple silk velvet pillow of the right size will have a remarkable effect on a damask sofa because of the combination of scale and texture. Pillows with a contrasting banner-style band or those with giant pearl or horn buttons read like miniature roomscapes in their own right within a furniture grouping, especially as I layer them, one upon the other onto the additional texture of the upholstery.

Silk velvet is a luscious fabric that always looks good when made up into plump pillows with bold fastenings, such as this big mother-of-pearl button. Silk velvet with damask, silk on silk, and silk on linen are all classic Kelly Hoppen combinations.

The plainest of fabrics, such as a natural, tightly woven linen, makes an excellent pillow when designed with a smart foldover that is finished with a large-scale button. The impact comes from the simplicity and contrast between the linen and the horn button.

This pillow is made from plain natural linen with a pair of slim contrasting silk-velvet banners. It is a charming but restrained look in conjunction with the leather dining chair. The shape and size ensure that the pillow will not slip off the chair.

Linen is one of my favorite fabrics, and I use it in all my designs in some way. Here I have overlaid black lace to create a beautiful new texture that is sexy and lighthearted. Covering one pillow halfway emphasizes the delicacy and the playful effect.

A double-layered banner detail runs around this linen pillow—one in the same linen as the main cover and the other in contrasting silk velvet. This pure combination is perfect in relation to the leather upholstery on a bench at my dining table.

Pillows in contrasting materials have a lively spirit, as shown in this combination of taffeta and linen pillows aligned on the Villa sofa by Donghia, which is upholstered in velvet and Novasuede. The proportions are perfect—the smaller pillows in front are just shy of half the size of the larger ones—resulting in a very comfortable seat. Within this vignette, the straight lines are beautifully balanced by the circles of the Ring Screen, which I designed, and the curved crystal lamp.

This is an exciting and graphic arrangement, with the square lines of the sofa and pillows in play with the Ring Screen. There is a strong distinction between the front and back pillows, which combine taffeta, linen, and rectilinear mother-of-pearl buttons.

The vintage chair in my bedroom was re-covered with mohair velvet from Fox Linton—a glorious, touchable texture. To enhance the sensuality, I added a slimline ivory silk-velvet pillow finished with two characteristically large pearl buttons.

*For me, pillows embody the textural quality and comfort in the room as a whole; they reflect and complement all the other elements within it.*

# DRAPES

**Like many aspects of interior design, drapes have evolved into a simpler form of their former selves, and window treatments are often more about letting light in than keeping it out.**

I have long preferred sheer drapes to those that are lined and interlined—they also create privacy because sheer drapes allow light into your rooms, while blocking the view to outsiders passing by—but every type of drape has its place and it is, of course, down to personal preference. This will depend not only on your room, but on what feeling you want to create.

The art of designing good drapes is in choosing the right fabric with the right texture and hanging them on the right pole for the room. Drapes form a backdrop and a contrast for objects and furniture. Choose fabric with this in mind because everything must connect and be in harmony. Make sure that the fabric you choose will be tactile and fluid on the window. The best way to do this is to purchase large samples so that you can see how the cloth will hang. Everyone has a view on length—I like drapes to pool on the floor. I use a lot of poles from McKinney and Co., which are among the best, and there is an excellent line of finials, both off-the-shelf and custom-made. Sometimes I use the plainest wrought-iron poles with no finials at all— the rule for me is, the simpler the better.

Borders and banners always make their way into my designs. The vertical banner is just an extension of the horizontal runner, both of which were inspired by the Japanese obi belt on a kimono (an example of something I have seen and turned into a creative idea for a completely different application). I am also intrigued by what you can do with ripping and shredding fabrics—the textural result is charming.

## KELLY'S *TOP PICKS*

SHEER DRAPES in linen or scrim that let light into the room, but provide privacy

UNLINED DRAPES that hang and fold in a soft, tactile manner

HEMS THAT BRUSH THE FLOOR with a kink, like an Italian man's pants

*Top row:*
**SHEER LINEN DRAPES** (*left*) with a wonderful crisp texture pool onto the floor, adding softness to the living space. Windows hung with sheer fabrics create a greater sense of connection to the outside.

**A DOUBLE LAYER OF PARACHUTE SILK** (*center*) hangs from soft pleating on a plain wrought-iron pole. The fabric drapes in a fluid manner and pools beautifully onto the floor.

**CRISPLY PLEATED SHEER LINEN** (*right*) falls into folds on the floor, allowing diffused light into the space and a view to the garden. The Jielde floor lamp is from Caravan.

*Bottom row:*
**WHITE SHEER COTTON DRAPES** (*left*) hang in my living room, on either side of a central shade with a broad band of carpet webbing as a graphic banner detail.

**SHEER METALLIC LINEN** (*center*) was my choice for these drapes because of both the texture of the fabric and the sheer chic of the look.

**RIPPING OR SHREDDING** (*right*) is as charming as it is unconventional. I have used it here on the most basic linen scrim in Stephen Webster's flagship jewelry store. I love the contrast between the linen damask upholstery and the irreverence of the slashed fabric.

# MEDIA

**I love television, love watching movies, and love being entertained, so it is no surprise that I love seeing the television screen either fully on display or smoothly integrated into the room.**

For years designers, including me, have been asked to hide away the television set in discreet cabinets. In some instances this is still the right approach, but I much prefer to see the screen and so do the majority of my clients, so I tend to design its installation to be very much a central part of the room. It is a definite fact of life that a room with a television in it will be used far more than a room without one.

Televisions belong in the family room, study, kitchen, and bedroom, and more and more I am asked to put them into the bathroom. They can be behind sliding screens, in cabinets, and behind closet or cupboard doors, and some people like the television to pop up out of a cabinet at the end of the bed.

I use specialist media consultants for all my television installations, and I would strongly advise you to do the same. An installation that is any more complex than mounting a flat screen onto a wall or having your television fixed on a wall-mounted arm will require a professional eye for both the detail and the technology.

If you are undertaking a major renovation that includes rewiring, take the opportunity to incorporate integrated sound and vision systems that are linked throughout the house because this will give you far greater freedom in creating a sleek installation. It will also add to the value of your home, as well as giving you a great deal of pleasure.

**THE TELEVISION SCREEN IS INTEGRATED** (*opposite, top and bottom*) into a wall of ebonized shelving in this cozy living space. The electronic sliding screen has been designed as a fabulous vertical banner that runs from floor to ceiling—it is a joy of a design because you have the option of seeing the television or not, and either way it looks just as good. Above all, a living room such as this must be not only formal for when you entertain, but also supremely comfortable so that you can truly relax.

**THIS TELEVISION INSTALLATION** (*left*) in a London townhouse is an extraordinary feat of technology and engineering. The screen is viewed through an enormous banner of black glass that is also the fireplace surround. It is a wonderfully witty twist on the classic fireplace with a mirror over the mantle because, in this instance, the entire chimney breast is a reflective glossy surface that surrounds the contemporary fireplace. When the television is switched off, you would never know it was there.

## TELEVISION CHECKLIST

▓ Wiring for televisions and multimedia systems must be thought through at the same time as all other wiring—this is the time to enlist professional help because integrated systems require technical know-how.

▓ A flat screen with wires chased (concealed) in the wall is the simplest type of installation, but you should still seek professional advice to make the most of your proposed ideas and system.

▓ Design the room to feel good and be truly comfortable. It will be used constantly and is for entertainment and fun.

# KELLY'S *TOP PICKS*

**CIRCULAR SHAPES** because they are feminine yin shapes that balance the masculine yang

**UPHOLSTERY** that is unmistakably unique, such as graffiti-print leather on an antique armchair, to create an unexpected piece

**ORGANIC FURNITURE,** especially a vintage piece such as this chaise, in stark contrast to the other items in the room

**CUSTOM-MADE LAMPS** that appear to be hand sketched into the room and therefore bring their own quirkiness into play in the space

DETAILS such as contrasting bands and dark buttons on glazed linen-damask machine-washed pillows

ENHANCING A ROOM with simple displays of fresh flowers and scented candles, which add another layer of flattering soft light

THE WIT of using a traditional method of upholstery in a modern way—such as leaving the X-shaped marker stitch as the finish, instead of stitching on the button

NATURAL LIGHT—for the effect it has on every surface and texture, as well as your mood

# BEDROOMS

YOUR BEDROOM IS YOUR ULTIMATE COMFORT ZONE,
AND IT SHOULD BE DESIGNED TO PLEASE ALL THE
SENSES. IT IS YOUR SANCTUARY—A PLACE TO CHAT,
READ, LIE DOWN AND THINK, REST, SLEEP, AND LOVE.

**THE COMFORTABLE AND LUXURIOUS** en-suite guest room in my home is a supremely calming space, where the all-white scheme is complemented by accents of chartreuse, metal, and black oak. I used Mirror Ball pendants by Tom Dixon in place of lamps to provide bedside light because I enjoy the quirkiness, proportion, and reflective effect. The bedspread and pillows were custom-made using cotton and linen fabrics, each with its own subtle texture that adds to the overall rich white tapestry. The contrasting chartreuse velvet banners align in a balanced albeit asymmetric fashion. The Mies van der Rohe Barcelona stool at the foot of the bed is a convenient place for overnight bags.

*Your bedroom is an intimate reflection of your personality and style—it is your private nest,* and a retreat from the rest of the world and all of its stresses. I ask my clients a series of extremely personal questions in order to create their couture bedrooms. Women are often the working-woman wonders of the family, multitasking their way through a range of roles, including that of hostess and mother. Men need their own space within a shared space because they invariably dislike jostling to get up and go in the morning. Do not make the mistake of thinking that the bedroom is less important than a principal living space because no one but family will see it. You will see it. What you touch and how you feel are perhaps more important in the bedroom than in any other space in the home because the design emphasis is on the feelings of protection and security.

What do you want to see when you walk into your bedroom? What impression do you want? Obviously, the bed will be the dominant feature of the room. Will it call to you with seductive overtures? Is your bed the right size and blissfully comfortable? The bed is your

## BEDROOM CHECKLIST

■ The bedroom is as important as the main living areas. It is your personal space, and the emphasis must be on luxury, comfort, peace, and security.

■ Define how the bedrooms will be used. Are they also dressing rooms and, in the case of children's room, are they study or den areas too? Make a list of priorities, in order to figure out what will work practically in the space.

■ Use fabrics in different textures, to build up a luxurious look for the bed—this is always successful when you use different tones of the same color.

**THE RESTFUL WHITE SPACE** (*left*) of my guest room has doors to the garden curtained with sheer white Sahco Hesslein fabric, the ideal choice to keep the textural quality flowing throughout the space and enhance the light, airy feel. The white wooden flooring brings warmth, while touches of metal— the trim on the bergère chair that I designed, the silver Bishop side table by India Mahdavi, the Tom Dixon lights, and the Barcelona stool— add a dynamic quality.

**THE PERFECT TONAL PITCH** (*opposite*) is achieved by upholstering the Frou Frou bed by Promemoria in velvet that blends with the wood-lined walls and works well with the velvet bedspread because each element is in the same tone of color. The taupe leather Gacy armchairs by Promemoria bring in more texture, and the white bedside lights and the wall light by Conciluce add the right touch.

## KELLY'S *TOP PICKS*

SCULPTURAL pendant lights suspended on either side of the bed

LUXURIOUS BEDSPREADS that feel marvelous against the skin

CONTROLLABLE, SUBTLE LIGHTING that helps to create a harmonious and peaceful bedroom

A BEAUTIFUL, SOFT CARPET in silk, lambswool, or sheepskin, which brings warmth to the space and feels wonderful under bare feet

THE WOW FACTOR OF THIS ROOM (*above*) lies in the sheer scale, tempered by the subtlety of tone and texture. The bed is my own design, made with "sueded" buffalo, which has also been used on the border of the rug. The star element is the pair of Spina crystal chandeliers, hung at lamp position on either side of the bed, to give the space sophistication.

main piece of furniture, and you have many options to consider for the headboard and base, the styling on a four-poster (if that is your choice), the bedcover and pillows (see page 184). You may have to design your bedroom for more than the purpose of sleeping. Will it also function as your dressing room, study, and perhaps even the place where you watch television?

The master bedroom embraces sleep, seduction, and safety. It is a very interesting place to design for a woman because she is perhaps a mother, sex symbol, partner, and professional. The dressing room is often part of the bedroom by being integral or set off to one side in a dedicated room. This is where you dress for your performance in life, metaphorically speaking, setting the stage for your day. You can envisage who you want to be that day, and dress for your audience in the outside world.

Children's bedrooms are as personal to them as yours is to you. Respect that and give them the chance to create their own space, based on how they like to feel in their private world (see page 188).

The guest bedroom is a bit more of a show-off than the principal bedroom, but it mirrors who you are in the same way that the master bedroom does, and should, therefore, be appointed with attention to luxury and use. For me, the overriding aim of the guest room must be that when friends leave, they feel as if they have just had their best night's sleep.

As ever, your design tools are the grid and mood boards (see pages 63 and 98–99). Work with both to reach the point where your design crystallizes as you refine your ideas, costs, and compromises. Encourage your children to create their own mood boards; both you and they will learn a great deal, and the resulting room will be a far more successful space.

### Lighting

The lighting scheme must be planned at the earliest stage, to see what existing circuitry can be utilized and what additional light sources are needed. At the very least, you should install dimmer switches to control light levels to suit your activity. Bedside lights

**BUTTONED UPHOLSTERY** (*left*), perceived as a traditional aesthetic, looks fresh and modern on both the bed and headboard. The vintage linen has a delightfully organic texture that is in contrast to the clean lines of the room— the navy accent linen on the pillows smartens the effect. The look is completed by the Andrew Martin steel chests topped with chic lamps of my design.

**SIMPLE LUXURIOUS COMFORT** (*below left*) has been achieved in this relatively small bedroom. The gridlike headboard increases the sense of space, while the silk-velvet bedspread immediately adds a luxe touch. The Archimedes desk lamps from Andrew Martin make practical bedside lamps and give the room a "sharpening" edge that works with the nickel globe ceiling light from Robert Clift Lighting.

are critical—not just because they are used for reading, but because they are also a sculptural presence that add personality to the overall picture.

## Flooring

My last consideration in terms of raw materials in the room is the flooring. By the time I choose the floor, I know the wall finish (usually white waxed plaster because I love the look) and all the furniture and fabric tones and textures (see page 186). I am using more and more wood, for it is warm and organic, but more often than not you are barefoot in the bedroom, so a silk or shag-pile carpet or rug is a blessing under your feet, looks incredibly luxurious, and can zone the floor to the bed or seating area.

## Design solutions: My bedroom

In my Georgian townhouse I have a smallish bedroom, but the size did not impede me in creating a space that has everything I want. The bed has built-in side units for water, books, glasses, pens, and paper. The dressing room is housed behind the exquisite dark wooden shoji doors that run from the bedroom into the landing and on into the bathroom. This was an extremely successful technique for connecting the spaces and maximized every inch, and I love the look and practicality of the solution. No bedroom will be peaceful if it is messy.

Design your room so that everything has its place—from clothes to belts, shoes, and bags, from his suits, shoes, and ties to your sports gear and the rest.

I design all my bedrooms to have a summer and a winter look, and I achieve it instantly by changing the bedspread from velvet to linen or damask, and vice versa, to reflect the seasonal shift or even my frame of mind. Some people have summer and winter drapes, but I prefer shutters because I like to wake with daylight filtering through the top of the window, and I enjoy the fact that you can have light, but no one can see you. I have a Spencer Fung dressing table that has been with me for a long time, and I think every woman should have a dressing table. I use it to display treasured items that spark memories and add soul to the room.

## Finishing touches

No one ever expresses surprise when I tell them to buy the best bedding and bed linen that they can afford. Pure linen sheets feel great, as do high-thread-count cotton sheets. For me, bed linen is white, white, white and can be combined with vintage pillowcases and top sheets that have embroidery or initialing, but you can mix textural weaves, patterns, and colors to suit your taste. The final layer in a bedroom is scent. Flowers, room perfume, fresh air, and clean linen are invaluable in contributing to your sense of well-being.

*No bedroom will be peaceful if it is messy. Design your room so that everything has its place.*

**CHALET BEDROOMS** (*left and opposite*) each have their own character, but you know they belong in the same home because of the specific tonal and color quality within each room, with the unifying wood cladding used throughout. Each also shares the superluxurious combination of texture in the throws, pillows, drapes, and carpets. Hanging bedside lights from the ceiling is a graceful and serene treatment because it contributes to the balance and symmetry of the room. It is also a practical solution because the bedside surfaces are left free for books and other accessories.

# KEYNOTES FOR A SUCCESSFUL BEDROOM

**Make your bedroom an intimate reflection of you because it is the ultimate private comfort zone and should please all the senses.**

Above all, design your bedroom to feel peaceful and secure. The bed will be the dominant piece, so use mood boards more carefully to create layers of lush textures, and consider having one bedspread for summer and another for winter. Closets must be designed to store all your clothes, shoes, and accessories. Lighting must be controlled at the bedside with at least two circuits, so that you can alter the mood from brighter dressing light to a quieter, more seductive level. The carpet should be your last consideration because it is the finishing layer of color and texture.

**THE BED** will be the centerpiece in the room, so consider not only its comfort and look, but also its proportion within the space. Low, wide headboards such as this create a streamlined effect, and the integrated bedside units provide plenty of drawers and bedside surface space.

**STORAGE** is a key part of any bedroom or dressing room and must be well designed to provide ample space to keep all your clothes, shoes, and accessories neat. Built-in closets give the most streamlined effect, and the interiors can be customized to suit your particular storage needs.

**LIGHTING** must be controllable from the bed, as well as the doorway, and there should be a minimum of two circuits, in order to set the light levels for different moods.

**BEDSIDE LAMPS** are an essential element and can make a significant style statement. These Anglepoise lamps from Ralph Lauren are an unexpected choice, but they are fantastic reading lights and a wonderfully linear, modern option.

**SHUTTERS** are a chic window treatment, as well as being practical—you can close them to the extent you wish, and they softly filter daylight.

**FURNITURE** is another layer of comfort within a bedroom. A bench at the end of the bed is good for getting dressed or can be used as a clotheshorse. Dressing tables are every woman's essential in my view, and a vintage chair will sit like a piece of art.

**THE VIEWS OF MY BEDROOM** (*opposite*) illustrate how a smallish room can contain all you need and still retain its sense of space. The taupe palette is accented with black and brought alive with the mix of textures—velvet, linen, silk, and shag-pile carpet. I have two different looks for the bed, which I change to reflect the seasons. At night, concealed lighting gives the room a warm, seductive glow.

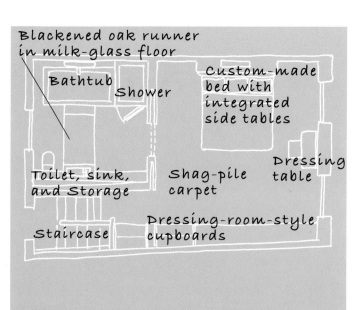

# BEDS, HEADBOARDS, AND PILLOWS

**The bed is the main piece of furniture in your bedroom, so make sure it looks as good as it feels, with an upholstered padded headboard and layers of textural covers.**

There is a vast choice of bed frames, bases, and headboards, and the styling options for the bedcovers and pillows are almost infinite. Start by choosing a fabric for the bedspread that feels delicious to sit and lie upon, then make a decision for the headboard and base. I tend to use the same material on the headboard and base of a bed—linen, velvet, leather, faux suede, satin, cashmere, or perhaps fur—then I add one or perhaps two more fabrics into the mix for the throw pillows, depending on the choice of fabric for the bedspread, to achieve a harmonious elegance. The number of pillows that some people use has been said to ruin sex lives because you are always fighting to get past them and onto the bed. In my view, four to six pillows achieves the right look, comfort, and practical balance.

The pitch of design in a bedroom will always be about texture and layering and building up the story to create an image of calm and a peaceful mood. The more confident you become, the more you can step outside your own box, but be aware that too many fabrics can suddenly jar the eye and read as confused or contrived. One of the things I always visualize, then ultimately see in reality, is a pretty view of the room to the left, to the right, forward and back, from whatever standpoint.

*Opposite, clockwise from top left:*
**LAYERING** a small oblong ivory linen pillow with a silver silk-velvet band in front of a large taupe velvet one is a great look and extremely comfortable; the larger pillow is deeper and more supportive.

**SUBTLE TONES** of taupe and gray linen and glazed raffia fabrics have been used on the headboard and pillows, which are finished with horn buttons.

**A BRAVE MIX OF FABRICS** from different houses—here silk velvet, natural linen, and damask from A One Fabrics, Busby & Busby, and de Le Cuona—for the pillows and bedspread will achieve an overall picture of textural perfection.

**CUSTOM-MADE PILLOWS AND BEDSPREADS** can be as pared down as these, to the point where the design relies on texture and the combination of "spot" and "stripe" in relation to the gridlike padded headboard.

*Above, clockwise from top left:*
**CHIC BANNER-STYLE PILLOWS** have been a key part of my designs from the beginning, and these classic two-tone linen versions are part of my line.

**SUCH SUBTLE TONES** of pinkish and grayish taupe are brought to life through the combination of fabrics—metallic linen, a shaggy finish, and velvet—with big mother-of-pearl buttons as the final layer of texture.

**A TEXTURAL PLEASURE** on both the eye and the skin, these layered pillows in a combination of linen, faux leather, and ribbed knit are plainly chic, as well as comfortingly warm.

**A STUNNING GLAZED LINEN**, such as the soft pinkish gray of this pillow, adds just the right amount of sparkle to the velvets and linens on this bed.

# BEDROOM FURNITURE

**Bedrooms not only need to look and feel fantastic, they must also be practical and user-friendly, with plenty of good storage, to keep your belongings in an orderly fashion and allow you to find things and perform tasks with ease.**

Any bedroom needs some furniture other than the bed and bedside tables. What you choose depends on your space and whether or not you want to create a miniature living area within your bedroom. Most of us have room for a chair, even if it only ever gets used as a throw-zone for clothes. This could be a charming vintage piece or a revamped inherited antique. Interiors stores have many delightful options ready to go, but you can create so many looks simply and easily with new upholstery on chairs and covers on pillows—timeless luxury with suede, cashmere, and wool; masculine crispness with leather and damask; soft femininity with velvet and satin. Linen is an all-time great fabric that meets all the requirements when it comes to creating any chic, contemporary look.

Plan your bedroom according to your habits and needs, so that if you like reading there, you can access a seat, rather than having to lie on the bed (unless that is what you prefer). I have a dressing table and advise my clients to do likewise; there is nothing nicer than having a dedicated place for jewelry and treasures.

Bedrooms are perfect for mirrors. Far more than a reflective surface, they bounce light into and around the room and can be leaned against walls like artworks.

## KELLY'S *TOP PICKS*

**BEDS** with padded and upholstered headboards and layers of textures in the form of pillows and throws on top of high-thread-count white bed linen

**TRUNKS OR CHESTS** as bedside tables

**VINTAGE CHAIRS** that have been upholstered in a luxe fabric and finished with an interesting trimming and pillow

**DRESSING TABLES** to display personal items, photographs, and jewelry

**MIRRORS** to reflect light around the room

**A DRESSING TABLE** (*left*) is the perfect place for a woman to sit and finish dressing. I keep costume jewelry and other treasured items on my Spencer Fung dressing table.

**METAL CHESTS** (*bottom left*) make quirky bedside tables that double up as storage boxes. I love the contrast between the slub texture in the linen pillows and bedcover and the sheen of the metal.

*Opposite, clockwise from top left:*
**A METAL FRINGE**, together with the white linen upholstery, has transformed the chair in my spare bedroom, and allows a witty glimpse of its nicely turned legs. The chartreuse velvet pillow with white linen band is pure Kelly Hoppen.

**THIS GLORIOUS VINTAGE CHAIR**, found at an antiques fair three years ago and reupholstered in mohair velvet from Fox Linton, is the star piece of furniture in my bedroom.

**EMPEROR'S YELLOW** is a favorite of mine, and I love it on this modern chair with tonal upholstery studwork. It makes a strong yet calm statement in conjunction with the multicircle mirror.

**BLACK DAMASK UPHOLSTERY** gives a contemporary twist to this Louis-style chair. The mirror behind it reflects the room, doubling the sense of space.

# CHILDREN'S BEDROOMS

**Children's bedrooms are often the only space in the house that they can really call their own, and they usually have very strong views about it.**

In design terms, as well as in life, you will get a better result if you respect this and give children the chance to create their own space, based on how they like to feel in their private world.

For most children, especially those aged from ten to sixteen, a bedroom is a place to sleep, play, do their homework, and hang out with their friends—in other words, it is where they like to spend a lot of their time. The space needs to be designed in such a way that it is flexible enough to allow them to do all of these activities and timeless enough that they do not outgrow it too quickly.

I ask children from as young as seven years old the same kinds of questions as I ask their parents, and I encourage them to put together tear sheets from magazines that give an impression of the things that they like. I translate them to mood boards to show them how their vision will come together once designed, in exactly the same way as I do for every other room in the house. It is amazing what you can learn from children, and most have a clear idea of what they want, especially the type of bed—which is often a bunk bed or a high bed with drawers and compartments, secret cubby holes, and space for their friends to stay over.

**SERIOUSLY COOL** (*above right*) ebonized bunk beds and plenty of built-in storage are a key feature of this boy's bedroom. The grid is subtly in play with the horizontal and vertical lines of the woodwork, echoed by the indigo banding around the linen bedspread and the single banner running through the Roman blind. The circular chair balances the strict masculine lines.

**THE SIMPLE, ORGANIC APPROACH** (*right*) that was taken in this room is reflected in both the color and the textures used. The Tom Dixon copper pendant light is the perfect sharpening contrast to the gray and ivory woods and the soft textures of the bedcovers and pillows. As this is the kids' room in a ski chalet, the space has been used to capacity, with three custom-made beds.

## KIDS' ZONE CHECKLIST

- Communication is key. Talk to your kids to find out what they really want in their rooms. You will learn a great deal and create a better design.

- Create inspiration boards and translate them into mood boards with your children to crystallize their vision of the space. This also gives you a great starting point for discussion.

- Work with their ideas within the grid, and make as much of a play on texture and color as you can when choosing materials and furnishings.

- Avoid trendy or branded ideas because they date with lightning speed.

- Design the room to evolve with your child as he or she grows up, so that your investment in the room is long-term.

**THE COMBINATION OF SOFT SHELL PINK AND WHITE** (above) in this girl's bedroom is timeless because it will "grow up" as she does. Floating shelving such as this looks just as good filled with toys as it will when used to store handbags and other accessories later in life. The upholstered detail that runs around the full L-shaped headboard makes the bed work as both a bed and a sofa.

**LINEN IS A STAR FABRIC IN EVERY WAY** (right), and here Hungarian ticking linen on the headboards and eiderdowns in this English country bedroom gives a gentle kind of chic that is perfectly modern. Semisheer linen drapes have a finishing band in strong orange, which adds a bit of zip to an otherwise neutral scheme.

*For most children, a bedroom is a place to sleep, play, do their homework, and hang out with their friends—it is where they like to spend a lot of their time.*

## BEDROOM LIGHTING KEYNOTES

Dimmers are an absolute must because you can raise or lower lighting levels to suit your mood and different occasions.

A preset system will let you select different lighting scenes at the touch of a button.

**AN ARRANGEMENT OF GLASS PENDANT DROPS** (*left*) by Bocci hangs on either side of this bed. They add a delicate and feminine touch to the room, as well as providing essential bedside lighting.

**EXQUISITE CRYSTAL CHANDELIERS** (*below left*) by Spina are in stunning textural contrast to the plaster wall, sueded buffalo headboard, and silk-velvet pillows. I love using chandeliers in this unexpected way, hung low in pairs on either side of a bed.

**CIRCULAR SHAPES** (*above right*) are in play here, with the iBall chair and Neblina chandelier from Jerry Pair. The effect is like a cluster of flowers suspended cloudlike from the center of the ceiling.

**WHERE SPACE IS TIGHT** (*right*), a pendant light makes a great alternative to a bedside lamp. The iconic Copper Pendant Lamp by Tom Dixon casts a warm pool of light, and its reflective surface adds to the textural melting pot in this bedroom.

# BEDROOM LIGHTING

**It is how you use the combination of light types that will give you the variation of light within a bedroom and, ultimately, a successful scheme.**

Imagine light that casts into pools to illuminate exactly what you want to emphasize—an object or artwork, the texture of a dark oak floor, polished-plaster wall, or even a luxe bedcover. Keep that image in your mind as you plan your bedroom lighting.

As with any room, you will always need more lighting than you think, especially in the winter, so plan for a number of different circuits to give you maximum flexibility. The more lighting you have, the more choice you have to create the mood you want.

Think carefully about the positioning of lights and the type of light they create to ensure you create the right balance. Remember, reflected light will bounce off glossy and mirrored surfaces, whereas it will softly glow on polished or other soft surfaces, such as wood and plasterwork. Darker finishes absorb more light, so you will need about 20 percent more lighting to achieve the optimum balance in the room.

**THE HORIZONTAL WALL LIGHT** (*left*) by Conciluce above the Promemoria bed gives this bedroom just the right seductive glow of light. Above the headboard are two discreet adjustable reading lights.

**IN A WITTY TAKE** (*below left*) on Hollywood-style mirror lights, a pair of up-scaled vertical panels with integral lights creates a flattering and balanced light for a dressing table.

**SUSPENDED BEDSIDE LIGHTS** (*below*) leave the surface beside the bed free for objects. This decorative pendant, from a department store, highlights a glass bowl, while ceiling lights set into the wood cladding are angled to wash soft light over the plaster wall behind the bed.

# signature
## KELLY'S DETAILS
# BEDROOM DRAPES

Drapes should never be designed in isolation from the other elements in the room—they must be thought out, so that they are as much a part of the whole as any other component of the scheme. You can have enormous fun with drapes—they can be lined, unlined, layered with other drapes or shades, and with simple or elaborate headings—and I am often surprised at how uninspiring some can be. The fluidity and fall of the fabric are key to drapes having "hang," and once you have decided whether or not to block out light or let it filter in through the fabric in the morning, really play around with your ideas to create something unique and perfect for your bedrooms.

A layered window treatment gives a terrific effect and is very much my way of having the best of both worlds. The sheer white linen drapes, with a wide silk-velvet band at the bottom, fall into a pool on the floor. They draw across a flat-weave taupe linen shade, to create a look that feels both young and light. The decorative sheer linen tie is one of my classic designs and unifies the two elements of the window treatment.

Think through every detail of the drapes, especially how they will meet and hang on the pole—here textured voile has been formally pleated, and the drapes are hung on a pole with a marvelous glass ball-shaped finial from McKinney and Co.

Both cozy and opulent, these silk-velvet drapes with a relief-swirl pattern hang over a flat-weave linen shade in this wood-clad bedroom—a fabulous contrast of materials. The decorative tie is of woven carpet tape, which brings in more subtle texture.

Subtle color shifts can be created by hanging one sheer linen over another, as I have done in this bedroom. I enjoy the way the fabric falls loosely and naturally into these random pleats—it feels relaxed while still being luxurious.

Lacelike white drapes that look entirely modern allow a beautiful diffuse white light into this basement bedroom. The Sahco Hesslein fabric is like a lattice of cotton threads that create their own geometric pattern within the space.

Deep horizontal bands of contrasting chartreuse velvet on lined linen drapes with an embroidered leaf motif not only improve the proportions of the wide window, but also add the punch of accent color to this bedroom.

The problem of bright light entering this ski chalet bedroom has been solved by a blackout shade flanked by lined natural linen drapes with a wide band of crimson velvet. The contrast in tone and texture is bold and delightful.

My spare bedroom has the prettiest white lacelike cotton drapes, which filter a flattering soft light into the room while still retaining privacy. The weave of this fabric emphasizes the circular shapes found elsewhere in the room—in the orb-shaped vase of farmed coral on the sculptural silver Bishop side table by India Mahdavi and in the artwork by Julie Cockburn on the wall above.

A band of red linen on natural linen scrim shows how the same design idea can work in a completely different way—here light filters into the room through the open weave of the fabric, and the look is young and informal.

# CLOSETS AND DRESSING ROOMS

**A beautifully designed dressing room is a most regal space. Keep it simple and practical, and put some love into the detailing.**

Dressing rooms and walk-in closets can be separate, dedicated spaces, designed with enclosed doors or devised to have open shelving and hanging compartments. Dressing spaces can be an extension of the bedroom if they run along the length of the room out into the hall or onto the landing, or they can be built within your bedroom as beautiful floor-to-ceiling closets. Your options are always dependent on available space.

I treat dressing rooms and closets with the same attention as kitchens because they have to be workable, with sufficient space for all your things. You have to decide where to have your underwear, socks, ties, T-shirts, sweaters, shoes, and so on; what will be folded and what will be on hangers. In most instances, the attention is on the closet fronts. Sliding doors work well in any space, whether detailed as shoji screens or designed in panels of contrasting materials; they are often the best option in smaller rooms because they take up less space by not opening into the room.

A mirror that gives you both a back and a front view is ideal, and good lighting is essential, especially on dark winter mornings. It is also convenient to have a chair or bench on which to throw your clothes when you undress at night.

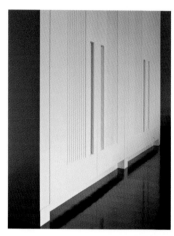

**THESE THREE DETAILS** (*left*) illustrate the bold, clean lines of floor-to-ceiling closets, one of which has sliding doors to get the most from the space (*near left*). Recessed handles set into the wooden doors are a practical modern detail, while the floating metal handles (*far left*) create a grand textural contrast with the ebonized wood.

**MIRRORS SET INTO THE CABINETRY** (*below left*) in this large dressing room create infinite reflections. The ebonized wood doors have been detailed with a horizontal shagreen banner and mother-of-pearl handles. This look is very me, not just for the textural contrast, but also for the sheer luxury.

**THE CHOICE OF HANDLES** (*below*) can make a door. These horn and nickel handles from Ochre on a suede-clad closet are one of my favorite combinations.

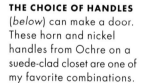

**THE SLIDING DARK-STAINED WOOD DOORS** of this dressing area make the most of the narrow space. The run of closets breaks in the center, to create an integrated dressing table. The recessed door handles run in line with the horizontal-line detailing, which keeps the design flowing. I always think you should have a bit of fun, and the sheepskin chair cover is a perfect example of how you can transform a simple piece of furniture with clever upholstery.

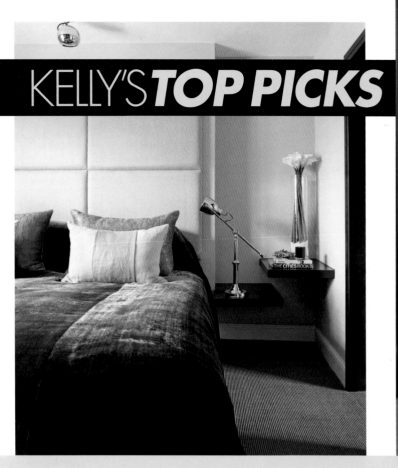

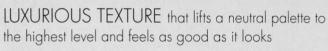

**LUXURIOUS TEXTURE** that lifts a neutral palette to the highest level and feels as good as it looks

**OPEN STORAGE** that acts as a room divider to separate the sleeping zone from the rest of the bedroom

**FURNITURE** other than the bed and side tables, such as this Martin chair from Casamilano, upholstered in Alma leather

**ATTENTION TO DETAIL**—the contrasting color and texture give a twist to this Hungarian linen headboard

**VINTAGE PIECES** such as my reupholstered 1960s metal-framed chair—a marvelous design ingredient

**BEDSIDE LIGHTS** suspended from the ceiling to hang low over the side table, such as this Conciluce glass drop

**A DRESSING TABLE** for putting the finishing touches to your look—an essential item for every woman

**PILLOW BANNERS,** even in the simplest form, such as these taupe silk strips on white linen

# BATHROOMS

THE BATHROOM IS THE ONLY ROOM IN THE HOUSE WHERE YOU CAN LOCK THE DOOR AND CLAIM THE SPACE AS YOUR OWN. THE PRIVACY IN ITSELF IS A LUXURY. THE BATHROOMS I DESIGN FOR MY CLIENTS ARE CUSTOM-MADE AND ARE BASED ON THE JAPANESE BATHING CUSTOM—THE CEREMONY OF CLEANSING, FOLLOWED BY RELAXATION IN A HOT TUB.

**THE REFLECTIVE QUALITY OF GLASS,** together with superb lighting, creates a magical atmosphere in my bathing space. The Starlet bathtub by Bette has been inset into a milk-glass surround, which ties in with the adjacent glass shower enclosure. I have used KH2 faucets from my own line for Waterfront Bathrooms. They are mounted on a floating wall of marble, with lighting behind that defines the space and illuminates the area beautifully.

*The first step in bathroom design is to decide how many you need* and where to site them. Space for bathrooms is usually taken from other rooms; a section of a master bedroom may be given over to a wet room or bathroom, although mostly an adjoining room is turned into a bathroom, with a shower, bathtub, sinks, and toilet, perhaps with an interconnecting dressing room or space for a massage table. You might be able to accommodate a shower and separate toilet—which is often the configuration that men prefer, whereas women tend to favor big bathrooms with two sinks and good storage. Once you have defined your requirements, it is relatively easy to design a bathroom if you use the grid (see page 63), to see the potential of your space and work out what goes where. Taking a line from the door across the floor and up to the sink is always a successful option, as is a banner that draws your eye through the space from the window to the bathtub or shower. I favor bathing over showering, so my own bathrooms always have the bathtub at the center of the design.

Bathrooms are expensive, and invariably a large chunk of the budget will be used for the plumbing—for the constant flow of hot water or the right pressure for the shower. Consult a professional because a house will often need some new plumbing and changes to water systems in order to function to a high standard.

## BATHROOM CHECKLIST

■ At the planning stage, decide whether to bring music and/or television into the bathroom.

■ Take the advice of your contractor and structural engineer about water flow rates, bathtub sizes, weight loads, and tanking (waterproofing).

■ Tubs, sinks, and faucets are the room's accessories, so choose carefully.

■ The lighting design should incorporate three circuits: one for main directional light, one for task lighting at the sink, and the third for soft backlighting and low-level lights.

■ The final touches are as important here as in any other room, so where space permits, have inviting seating.

**FOUR VIEWS** of my own bathroom show how the room works as a whole. The grid line from the bathtub across the floor to the sink was taken in the form of a blackened oak banner set into taupe-colored milk glass because this centered the room and gave the bathtub prime importance. The grid lines are also in play in the way the cupboards flank the mirror and sink. The washstand and mirror, glass bathtub surround, and shower enclosure are all custom-made, and the backlit floating marble wall behind the bathtub was also specially made to my design. All the faucets and the black shutters are from my lines, and the white Bishop side table is by India Mahdavi. The lighting scheme was designed by Robert Clift and me. In addition to the backlit wall behind the bathtub, there is more concealed lighting behind the toilet and sink, again giving a soft, flattering light. Preset controls have been programmed to give several instant settings at the touch of a button. This bathroom illustrates just how the symmetry of line and mix of wood and glass textures create a luxurious and timeless statement that is very much my signature.

**THIS SIMPLE DESIGN** (*left*) incorporates a custom-made floating sink at one end of the room, with a toilet and shelves opposite, and a Rifra's Nest tub and luxurious glass shower enclosure at the other.

**THIS THEATRICALLY FURNISHED BATHROOM** (*below*) features a Calide double tub by Antonio Lupi, on a blackened oak runner set into the Thassos marble. The large space is beautifully balanced, with a shower on one side and floating sink unit on the other. The chairs and Meridiani ottomans were reupholstered with toweling fabric.

**A FULL-HEIGHT CUSTOM-MADE WALL UNIT** (*opposite*) characterizes this space, where recessed mirror cabinets are separated by linear frosted-glass lightboxes. The flooring, backsplash, and baseboards are in gray Foussana stone. The sink is by Antonio Lupi, and the faucets and shower head are from Dornbracht.

## Lighting

The challenge is to design the lighting to allow you to create different moods to suit all the things you will be doing in the bathroom. Separate circuits and a preset system enable you to have five or six instant settings. In the morning, the bathroom is where you get ready for the day—everything you need is on hand, and the light is appropriately bright at the sink. In the evening, it becomes a retreat, where you prepare for bed and wind down—balanced, controllable lighting will give a subtle, calming atmosphere. It always amazes me what good lighting can do for a room, which is why it must be the focus of bathroom design.

Fixed overhead lights cast unflattering downward shadows, so I use directional top lights and low-level spots or uplighters; in many cases the light source itself is concealed. Lighting is about balance. Think of the wave of light in the room; how it should glow at low level in the shower, giving an uplifting light. Ditto in the bathtub area, where the wall behind the tub can be backlit to create a surrounding glow. Concealed lighting is enormously successful because it gives a soft, sensual light that is very calming. Task lighting at the sink is essential for putting on makeup or shaving. A series of tiny wall-mounted spotlights, fixed horizontally or vertically onto the mirror, creates the desired effect.

## Texture

After light, texture is the main design tool in a bathroom. I use a maximum of three materials, one of which is mirror, plus the wall finish. Reflective milk glass—a painted foil-backed reinforced glass—is a fantastic alternative to marble for floors and shower enclosures. It comes in many colors, it is relatively easy to install, and it is less costly than most marble and stone composites. Textural combinations could be mirror with stone and wood, glass and wood, resin and marble, marble and wood, or wood and rubber (a good choice for children's bathrooms).

## Storage

Well-planned storage streamlines a room and can be integrated and balanced within the space in line with the grid. An entire wall could house shelves, cupboards, and concealed drawers. A cupboard on one side of a sink may hold the toilet with storage above; the one on the other side can be floor-to-ceiling storage. Your space and needs will determine your options.

# KEYNOTES FOR A SUCCESSFUL BATHROOM

**The elements that make up a bathroom—faucets, sinks, bathtub, cabinets, materials, and finishes—give the space its personality. Sublime comfort is the aim because this is the only room in the house where you can shut the door and look after yourself.**

While thinking about your hard surface materials, work with the grid (see page 63) so that you can make the most of the space and create the "lines" of the room, perhaps with a banner in a contrasting material that runs across the floor and up the wall. Next choose the fixtures, bearing in mind the textures and subsequent spirit of the room. Avoid overhead lights that will shine unflatteringly onto your head—my advice is always to work with a lighting consultant.

**Custom cabinets**
**Cabinet with integrated lighting**
**Double sinks**
**Stone flooring**
**Freestanding bathtub**
**Walk-in shower**
**Dressing room**

**MATERIALS** and their various tones and textures play a key role in creating the overall look of a bathroom and giving the space its point of interest. In this bathroom the standout material is the wonderful gray-veined Arabescato stone, which has been used on the floor and two walls. Its lively texture has been balanced by the soft gray plasterwork on two of the walls and the pared-down ebonized cabinets and streamlined shelves. The use of mirror on the cabinet, together with a selection of glass accessories and vases, provides a reflective lift.

**THE FLOW** of marble continues into the shower and is in beautiful contrast to the polished plaster wall. I often design the up-stand baseboards to match the floors, as I have in this case, because this continues the flow of line.

**LIGHTING** must be well planned and flexible to allow for different light levels and moods. Task light for shaving and putting on makeup has been integrated into the mirrored cabinets because this gives the right kind of light to see properly, while still being soft on the face. There are also directional spotlights on a preset control panel and low-level lights that are set to glow at night. The niche in the wall by the bathtub provides a convenient spot for candles, for a relaxing bathing experience.

**STORAGE** is essential to bathroom design because there is potential for all your things to get messy. Have on display only what you really want to see, and keep the rest hidden away.

**FIXTURES** are available in a vast choice of shapes and styles for all budgets. Research your options

thoroughly at specialist bathroom suppliers, to find the right tub, sinks, toilet, showers, and faucets to suit your needs. The bathtub should be the most comfortable and shapely you can find. Installing two sinks makes the morning rush much less stressful, and the vanity unit can incorporate all-essential storage. Here the simplest of round sinks and bathtub balance the lines of the room.

**FAUCETS** are sculptural art pieces and come in all styles, from the simplest of squared-off designs to elongated ceiling-to-sink versions—these are from my line for Waterfront Bathrooms.

**A TELEVISION** can be set into the bathside wall (*opposite, bottom left*), a luxury that is increasingly requested—in the same way integrated music is now a standard.

# THE WET ZONE

**Bathing is a joy—lying in the bathtub can be one of the most recharging, vital experiences when you give in to the relaxation of being alone behind closed doors in a supremely calming space.**

When working through your mood boards and considering the grid formation of the room, the choice of bathtub will naturally be a prime consideration. A bathtub is a large, heavy, expensive item, and you must make sure not only that it has the right look and comfort factor for you, but also that your floors can take its weight when it is filled. Discuss all this and the plumbing with your contractor; it may well be that you have to strengthen the floor joists and upgrade your existing water system to provide hot water for the bathtub, the shower, and the rest of the house.

Extraordinary architectural effects can be achieved by running a banner of contrasting materials through the space, so that the bathtub sits proud in the visual center of the room. The choice of materials can be in stark contrast, such as ebonized wood with white Thassos marble, or tonally textural, in ivory and sand-colored limestones. Mirror and glass are always welcome in a bathroom for their magical reflective qualities; I frequently use milk glass instead of stone for flooring, into which I set a classic black-stained oak runner for maximum dramatic effect.

**THE DESIGN OF THIS BATHROOM** (*opposite*) is all about lines, both subtle in the tiling and dramatic in the vertical charcoal banner that runs across the floor, up the bathtub surround, and up the wall behind the bathtub. The lines of the tub itself and the elongated faucet add to the effect. Two directional ceiling lights wash light downward onto the wall banner.

**A FABULOUS EGG-SHAPED FREESTANDING BATHTUB** (*below left, top*) made of Pietraluce resin gives the right yin balance to the otherwise strict yang design, which is reinforced by the floating shelves and the combination of white tile and ebonized wood.

**A SOFT-EDGED OBLONG BATHTUB** (*below left, bottom*) is comfortable in this relatively small bathroom. Touches of black in the shutter and door, along with the angular metal-framed mirror, all work together to achieve a good balance.

**TONAL MATERIALS** (*below*) can be just as dramatic as more contrasting finishes, as shown in this mix of taupe milk glass, black oak, beige and gray polished stone, and white stone resin tub.

## Showers

First and foremost, showering is a faster and more practical experience than bathing. The water pressure and hot-water capacity must be up to standard, otherwise the shower will not function properly. If you are having a "wet room" shower area, there are pitfalls that must be avoided, such as insufficient tanking (waterproofing) and drainage. Powerful showers can flood a room within minutes without correct outflow. Take your contractor's advice, and investigate the practical options before undertaking any grand design changes in the shower.

My advice is to keep the shower as simple, as practical, and ultimately as sculptural as possible within your space. Open-sided, walk-in showers are fabulous to experience, especially with a full blast of piping-hot water and plenty of space in which to splash around. Enclosed glass-box-style showers with flush doors are probably the most practical (and safe) of all the options, but again this will depend on your ideals and available space. If there is room, a quirky stool is a nice finishing touch as a place to perch and, where possible, create alcoves to place soaps and shampoo.

## PRACTICAL POINTERS

- Work with a plumbing engineer that you trust.

- Do as much research as you can by visiting specialist bathroom stores.

- Old and period properties do not take kindly to wet rooms because, invariably, the floors are never plumb and you need a solid surface to ensure that the joins are waterproof.

*Shower rooms need to be Zen—both calming and invigorating.*

**A LOVELY SUBTLETY** (*left*) has been brought into this walk-in shower by the central runner of River mosaic, which has been set into the dove-gray Carerra marble behind the custom-made reinforced-glass shower screen. The nickel wood-block-style stool is a charming and practical addition, and the towel rail is within easy reach.

## SHOWERS KEYNOTES

The matte and shine combination of stone and glass is timeless.

Mosaics, textured pebble-style tiles, and slabs of marble are excellent choices for a shower zone, but keep wood away.

**THE CURVED SHAPE** (*above left*) of this open shower, screened by a simple panel of clear glass, is repeated in the pure simplicity of the freestanding Boffi pipe. The mosaic tiling behind the water spout tones with the beige Scala limestone floor. The arrangement of ceiling lights follows the shape of the shower and washes the wall with soft lighting.

**AN OVERHEAD SHOWER SYSTEM** (*above right*) such as this one requires a large hot-water tank with a high output of water pressure. The textured pebble-stone tile walls are highlighted by the overhead lighting.

**A BOXED-IN GLASS SHOWER COMPARTMENT** (*left*) is supercool in a large bathroom where you need to separate a showering zone. The wave design of the white plaster finish inside the shower adds subtle pattern and texture to the room, with its taupe plaster walls and floor of white Thassos marble and black oak.

**QUIRKY TEXTURE** (*right*), such as this pebblelike River mosaic tile made of fragments of polished glass, is a finish I love—shown here with a shower system from my line.

# signature
## KELLY'S
## DETAILS
## BATHROOM SINKS

Sinks have evolved probably more than any other bathroom element—their design is a real art, and 99 percent of the sinks I install for my clients have been specifically designed by me, so they are unique to the project. They can be in stone, composite resins, ceramic, marble, or wood. But what makes a great sink, whether round, angular, or with a flow-through, open-lattice surface, is how it sits in the space and relates not only to the faucets, but to all the other elements in the space; the aim is for a balance of drama and harmony. Faucets are the main accessories, and I think of them as sculptures, a real point of focus and things of beauty.

Sinks and faucets must work together, as much for look as for practicality. Here I used the Slim Rifra composite sink with chrome faucets from my line for Waterfront, to work with the white Thassos marble walls and custom-made black oak floating shelves.

The organic oval shape of the ceramic Piper 2 sink from Antonio Lupi sits beautifully on the floating black oak countertop with matching undershelf. The understated MEM wall-mounted faucets are from Dornbracht. Integral incandescent lighting set behind frosted-glass panels in the custom-made mirrored cabinet creates a beautiful and flattering light.

The graphic square lines of my KH2 chrome wall-mounted faucets from Waterfront Bathrooms are in perfect harmony with this rectangular Less sink by Rifra. The sink's wide, flat rim is both practical and good-looking.

I particularly like the way this Boffi PH cylindrical sink stands within this slim space and the way it is in contrast with the lines of the antique French mirror. My versatile KH2 wall-mounted mixer faucets work with many different styles of sink.

Custom-made white composite sink units were formed to flow along one wall in this generous-sized bathroom. The black-stained oak drawers and matching floating shelves below give the space a simple, graphic quality, which also keeps the feeling light and easy. Above each sink is a custom-made mirrored cabinet with integral linear side lights. Simple steel sink faucets from Boffi complete the design.

The textural quality of this open-lattice black Siltec sink is wonderfully attractive, utterly simple, and perfect with the single-spout faucet—both from Toscoquattro. The mirrored cabinet with integral lighting was designed to be as simple as possible.

The warmth and textural interest created by Arabescato stone, specialist plasterwork, and black oak cabinets required the purest sink forms—here shallow circular white ceramic sinks from Rifra teamed with wall faucets from my collection.

## POWDER ROOMS KEYNOTES

Build up a sense of drama through the use of texture, scale, and lighting.

Try to include a coat closet and concealed storage for soaps and towels. Where space permits, a comfortable seating is a nice touch.

**A MONOCHROMATIC POWDER ROOM** (*left*), with soft-taupe plastered walls and ebonized wood and milk-glass floor, looks crisp and welcoming. A black banner running through the white chair balances with the floor. The bordered sheer shade filters light into the room, while retaining privacy.

**CHARCOAL AND SAND** (*above right*) are a classic combination that exudes chic. The lighting is sexy, low, and flattering, and the arum lilies in tall glass vases on the floor add just the right note of softness.

**WARM OAK AND SOFT WHITE** (*left*) are a perfect mix for this powder room, where the floor banner from the hallway continues through the space and up the wall. The ornate Squint mirror is perfectly balanced with the barrel shape of the Antonio Lupi sink.

**THE FANTASTIC CONTRAST** (*right*) between the polished red lacquered wall in the mirror reflection and the rough quality of the plasterwork on the walls and ceiling illustrates how powerful a simple combination of textures in a design can be.

# POWDER ROOMS

**Communal spaces such as powder rooms deserve the same level of attention as any other room, so do not design them as an afterthought.**

The powder room is the one room in the house where you can go to town, as it were, because this room does not necessarily have to fit in with the rest of the house. However, I could never, ever see it as a room for tastelessness or kitsch installations.

Powder rooms can be delightful spaces with textural wall finishes, soft, sexy lighting, and a play on scale—perhaps a giant mirror with a ceiling-to-sink faucet, as I have done in my own home. I like to add color, and one of the ways you can do this is to create a single wall in a spectacular finish—red lacquer, silver gilt, metallic mosaics, or colored polished plaster are all great options. Think of the faucets and sinks as being the standouts of the space and choose them for their sculptural qualities.

The lighting is as key in the powder room as it is anywhere else in the house. As always, position downlights carefully, so that they will not shine directly onto a person's head, and make sure that the lights are controlled by dimmers (see pages 88–97 and 202). Remember the grid (see page 63), and pay special attention to the choice of flooring because floor banners work wonders on the proportions of a small space.

A single rare, beautiful object will never go unnoticed in a powder room, and your friends will appreciate the unexpected delight that such a detail adds. Flowers or little bowls planted up with greenery add both freshness and color, and can just as happily be placed on the floor as on the counter.

*Powder rooms can be delightful spaces with textural wall finishes, soft, sexy lighting, and a play on scale.*

**MY OWN POWDER ROOM** (*above*) is a slim space, and I emphasized this with both the vertical banner-style mirror and dramatic ceiling-to-sink faucet from Gessi, with controls from my line for Waterfront. The custom-made carved marble sink is installed wall to wall, and the walls themselves have been finished with umber-toned polished plasterwork. The mirror reflects a scene of ceramic books set in a backlit alcove above the toilet.

# KELLY'S *TOP PICKS*

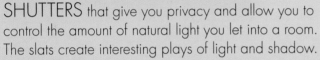

**SHUTTERS** that give you privacy and allow you to control the amount of natural light you let into a room. The slats create interesting plays of light and shadow.

**CONTRASTING** flooring materials to add interest and reinforce the grid in a room

**MIRRORS** that surprise and delight your eye by being in textural contrast to the other surfaces in a bathing space

**CLEVER STORAGE**, which may be concealed in glass-fronted cabinets or on show, such as this ebony drawer and floating shelf in an otherwise white scheme

TELEVISIONS, which can be installed in any room, in such a way as to be seamless within the design of the space

MILK GLASS, which is a spectacularly beautiful material—here there is an integral, beautifully lit display of farmed corals within a niche in the shower area

BANNERS AND RUNNERS, a perfect way to bring architectural drama and wow factor to any room

ONE-OFF SINKS that are totally unique—such as this one with a routed-out stone top in an organic cutout pattern

# DOWNTIME

YOUR TIME TO UNWIND OR
REV YOURSELF BACK UP.

**THE INCREDIBLE ARCHITECTURE** (*this page*) of this space, created by the circular staircase, is wondefully organic. The glass walls are finished with vertical natural oak sections and, with the other glass and marble, the textural quality is gentle and calming. Three giant spouts send an energetic flow of water into the pool.

**THE INDOOR-OUTDOOR FEEL** (*opposite*) is enhanced by the daylight that pours through the sliding glass doors. The gold mosaic steps are in stark contrast to the slate wall tiles and hardwood pool surround and ceiling. Up-down wall lights provide a subtle, flattering light.

# INDOOR POOLS, SAUNAS, AND HAMMAMS

**Increasingly, an indoor pool at home is a "normal" request. We spend so much more time at home, and home play zones, such as indoor pools, saunas, and hammam steam rooms, are the ultimate at-home luxuries.**

Sophisticated engineering allows us to burrow beneath our properties and add extra square footage. It is one of the most successful projects you can undertake because it adds enormous value to a home, not just in monetary terms, but in how you live and in what you can install—and your own indoor pool is probably the most luxurious of all.

I see all downtime spaces—the indoor pool, sauna, gym, and home movie theater—as rooms dedicated to different forms of relaxation. I think and meditate on the treadmill in my gym at home. Some clients ask for dedicated meditation spaces, while others relax with a glass of wine and a movie or music. I read in the morning, then exercise in my gym for an hour, which sets me up for the day. If I had my own pool I would swim, just as some of my clients do. At night I switch off from work for an hour or so by puttering around my house, moving this and that from one place to another, or I watch a movie. The whole idea of downtime centers on playtime at home.

Indoor pools, saunas, and steam rooms require an entirely different building principle and regular maintenance, so you must have specialist contractors. For instance, all indoor pools have air conditioning, in addition to a plant and control zone, and I always install top sound systems and, in some cases, large television screens. Exactly the same design principles apply in pools as in any other room. Textural and material contrast, flattering lighting, and a sense of theater and wow factor all combine to create a seriously cool "good mood" vibe.

**SUBTLE TEXTURED STONE WALLS** (*above*) that flow into the pool are grounded with a metallic mosaic banner that runs the length of this pool. The lighting is incredibly gentle—up-down wall lights are balanced with internal pool uplighting.

**A SIMILAR DESIGN IDEA** (*opposite top*) has been interpreted with soft gray stone slabs and mosaics in charcoal and eau de nil for a smart, masculine vibe.

**THIS SAUNA** (*right*) is beautifully balanced in the toning colors of wood used. Two cedar woods were chosen to distinguish the seating from the walls and ceiling.

**STEAM ROOMS, OR HAMMAMS** (*left and right*), based on Turkish baths, are fantastically luxurious additions to a home. I keep them absolutely sleek in looks and practical in terms of use, with very low lighting and an emphasis on surface texture. The simply designed hammam on the left is entirely made in silky-smooth pale limestone. The one on the right, which adjoins the glamorous pool above and ties in with it through the use of materials, is a strong mix of glossy charcoal mosaics with softly textured antique-style gray stone. These examples illustrate very different looks, yet all the textures used are lovely against bare skin.

**THIS HOME GYM** (*above*) is part of a complex that includes a pool, sauna, and movie theater. It is boxed within a glass compartment that does not interrupt the flow, and the textures in the entire area—wooden floors with plaster, stone, and glass walls—all work harmoniously. The mirror and table with water and towels are perfect touches.

**SPRUNG-WOOD FLOORS** (*left*) are an essential part of good gym design, and the mirrored wall opposite the equipment doubles the sense of space. For me, flowers can be brought into any space, to add a touch of organic life.

# GYM TIME

**Everybody wants to be fit, and more and more of us want to work out at home because it means we will actually do so more frequently.**

A good home gym needs space, air conditioning, and great equipment. It can be designed as a glass box within an excavated basement area or fitted into an existing room. There has to be enough space to do free weights, and I like to have lots of mirroring, to expand the sense of light and airiness—and also to see what I am doing.

I would always choose to have a gym over a spare bedroom or even an extra bathroom because working out in the gym each morning has become an essential part of my daily life. This is why making your wish list at the start of your design project is so crucial; it helps you to prioritize and create a more workable, livable home.

As well as being practical, a gym has to make you feel good because this encourages you all the more. I approach the decoration of a gym as I would any other room in the house. In addition to good-quality, good-looking equipment—a treadmill, stationary bike, and weight and kinesis machines—I hang large, beautifully framed photographs, perhaps add a quirky neon light (as I have done in my own gym), and bring in some color. In my gym there is a vintage Union Jack flag that provides color and fun, but in other gyms I might lean a decorative mirror

against the wall and have a series of planted sculptural pots. This kind of detail adds that feel-good factor.

Light your gym with care; you do not want to be on the yoga mat and have light shining in your eyes. I prefer lightboxes that shoot light upward—this is by far the most flattering light by which to work out because it is a gentle, round form of light that does not emphasize imperfections. A series of pendants is another good light treatment for the gym—and a way of bringing in a decorative, homey element—as long as they are positioned to suit how you will be using your space.

Final touches in gyms are bottled water, well displayed on a cool table; masses of neatly folded towels; and music, music, music.

**THE GYM IN MY OWN HOME** (*below left*) is just another room in the house to me and is decorated accordingly, with mirrors, pictures, and plants, so that I feel good while I am working out.

**A SERIES OF THREE GLASS PENDANTS** (*below*) is a charming treatment in a gym because it has the chic appeal of home, while being practical in the space. The series of infinity reflections that is set up by mirrors on all the walls is intriguing.

## KELLY'S *TOP PICKS*

**TECHNOGYM EQUIPMENT**—it performs well and also looks great.

**WALL-MOUNTED TELEVISIONS** and integrated sound systems

**LIGHTING** that shines upward and not into your eyes

**AIR CONDITIONING**—essential for every workout space

# PLAYTIME

**Dedicated grown-up playrooms may be furnished with a vast television screen, bar, jukebox, popcorn machine, table tennis and pool tables, and more.**

There is no better way to watch a movie or the sports channels than on a giant screen in your own home theater. The installation of a home movie theater has become common practice, and most of my clients see theirs as an extension of the family room.

A home movie theater consists of about eight chairs, depending on their size, a great screen, surround sound, and an atmosphere of complete and utter cozy comfort. It is having fun on a different level. It does not have to be in a large space, but it does have to be air-conditioned. The equipment pumps out heat and so do our bodies, so it is an essential consideration and any specialist will insist upon it—just as I insist that

you hire a specialist when installing a home movie theater. Walls can be acoustically treated, and floors should be carpeted to balance the sound, but from that point on, you are free to give in a little to the fantasies of what your screening room can look like. I have created rooms that have a glamorous 1930s flair and others that feel like a vast, luxurious bedroom in which you can happily curl up on pillows and throws of cashmere, silk, and lamb's fleece. Focus the design on rich, soft texture and the lowest lighting levels.

In a games room, the equipment will take center stage, with seating and your own version of comfort incorporated into the room's design.

**THE SCARLET VELVET** (*above*) gives the Meridiani Belmondo chairs and footstools a luxe feel. Between the seats are letter-shaped steel side tables by Andrew Martin— the six together spell out "MOVIES." The fabric-paneled walls are in the precise tone of the shag-pile carpet, giving a cozy feel. Glowing wall lights provide just the right level of light before the movie.

**THIS SAND- AND COPPER-TONED HOME MOVIE THEATER** (*opposite top*) has inviting Bogart daybeds by Meridiani, each with a scrumptious faux-fur throw. Floor lamps light each chaise, while wall lights provide soft, balanced light.

**GAME ON** (*right*) with this custom-made pool table, made to my design by Sir William Bentley Billiards—an excellent example of a modern organic piece. The wood looks like it is unfinished, which gives the table a quiet charisma within this grown-up playroom. Unfinished vertical oak sections clad the walls and emphasize the naturalness and calm ambience of the space— the inspiration for the table's design came as a result of my trip to Bhutan.

# ACKNOWLEDGMENTS

I would like to thank all my clients who have allowed me back into their homes to photograph the finished results—without them this book would not have been possible. A huge thank you also to my amazing interior design team, who executes every job with such love and precision. Special thanks to Lucy, Tania, Huei, Adam, Emma, and Dustin for being so passionate about your work—you are my backbone.

Thank you to Michael Lindsay-Watson and Peng Wang for always being there and acting as my second voice; to Leila Naghashi for keeping me sane and running my life for me; and to Pheobi, who takes care of me and my home, day in and day out.

Jacqui Small, thank you for everything—you are so much a part of the family now. Thanks to Sarah Stewart-Smith for interpreting my thoughts and putting them into beautiful words. Mel Yates, you have made photographing my work so easy—thank you for understanding my vision. Thank you to Lawrence Morton for your endless creative design and calmness; and to Zia Mattocks for editing the book with such care—especially for a dyslexic like me!

Rob Clift, thank you again for all your help and hard work with lighting. Thanks to John Carter for your amazing flower designs—you are so creative and a wonderful friend; to Hayley Newstead for your beautiful flower arrangements; and to Kim Pope for your constant creativity and hard work. Special thanks to both Doreen Scott and Thomson Schultz for making perfect soft furnishings and drapes, and to everyone else that we work with to create beautiful homes.

Finally, my thanks to the following resources, who form my "little black book" of ideas.

## ANTIQUES

**Alfies Antique Market**
www.alfiesantiques.com
**Portobello Road Antiques Market**
www.portobelloroad.co.uk
Every Saturday
**Sunbury Antiques Market**
www.kemptonantiques.com
2nd and last Tuesday of the month
**Talisman**
www.talismanlondon.com

## ART

**The Affordable Art Fair**
www.affordableartfair.co.uk
**Frieze Art Fair**
www.friezeartfair.com
**Michael Hoppen Gallery**
www.michaelhoppengallery.com
**Stephanie Hoppen Gallery**
www.stephaniehoppen.com

## BATHROOMS & KITCHENS

**Alternative Plans**
www.alternative-plans.co.uk
**KH for Waterfront Bathrooms**
www.waterfrontbathrooms.com

## ECO BUILDING

**Nick Skinner**
+44 (0)7904 017274

## FABRICS

**Abbott and Boyd**
www.abbottandboyd.co.uk
Fabrics and wallpapers
**Andrew Martin International**
www.andrewmartin.co.uk
Specialist fabrics
**A One Fabrics**
+44 (0) 20 8740 7349
Silk velvets and fashion fabrics
**Bennett Silks**
www.bennett-silks.co.uk
Silk and satin fabrics
**Casamance**
www.casamance.com
Contemporary fabrics
**The Cloth Shop**
www.theclothshop.net
**Colefax and Fowler**
www.colefax.com
Fabrics and wallpapers
**de Le Cuona** www.delecuona.co.uk
Linen fabrics
**Donghia** www.donghia.com
Textured fabrics
**Fox Linton** www.foxlinton.com
Sheer, silk, and suede fabrics
**JAB** www.jab.de

**J Robert Scott** www.jrobertscott.com
**Kravet** www.kravet.com
Contemporary furnishing fabrics
**Pedroso E Osório**
www.pedrosoeosorio.com
Sheers and linens
**Rubelli** www.rubelli.com
Specialist fabrics
**Sahco Hesslein** www.sahco.de
Linen and other fabrics
**Zimmer + Rohde**
www.zimmer-rohde.com
Sheer fabrics

## FENG SHUI

**Richard Ashworth**
www.imperialfengshui.info

## FIREPLACES

**B+D Design** www.bd-designs.co.uk
Custom-made fireplace sculptures
**Chesney's** www.chesneys.co.uk
All styles of fireplaces
**CVO Fire Ltd** www.cvo.co.uk
Modern fireplace installations

## FLOORS

**Bartholomeus** +32 50 212 227
**Borderline Carpet Planning
Service** www.borderlinecps.com
Natural carpets
**Byrock** www.byrock.co.uk
Resin flooring
**Crucial Trading**
www.crucial-trading.com
Natural flooring and carpets
**Dalsouple** www.dalsouple.com
Rubber flooring
**The Rug Compay**
www.therugcompany.co.uk
**Top Floor UK Ltd**
www.topfloorrugs.com
Rugs and wood floors

## FLOWERS & GARDEN DESIGN

**Absolute Flowers and Home**
www.absoluteflowersandhome.com
**Chris Moss Gardens**
www.chrismossgardens.com
Garden designer
**Columbia Road Flower Market**
http://columbiaroad.info
Every Sunday
**John Carter Flowers**
www.johncarterflowers.com
**Scent Floral Design**
+44 (0)20 8203 5458
Artificial flowers

## FURNITURE

**Andrew Martin International**
www.andrewmartin.co.uk
**B&B Italia** www.bebitalia.it
**Baltus** www.baltuscollection.com
**Casamilano**
www.casamilanohome.com
**Christian Liaigre**
www.christian-liaigre.fr
**Christopher Guy**
www.christopherguy.com
Contemporary and classic pieces
**European Design Centre**
www.edclondon.com
**La Fibule** www.lafibule.fr

**George Smith**
www.georgesmith.co.uk
Handmade furniture
**Gosling Ltd** www.tgosling.com
Custom-made pieces
**India Mahdavi**
www.india-mahdavi.com
**KH Furniture Collection**
www.kellyhoppenretail.com
**Meridiani** www.meridianisas.it
**Minotti** www.minotti.com
**Modenature** www.modenature.
com/www.kellyhoppenretail.com
**Poliform** www.poliformuk.com
**Promemoria**
www.promemoria.com

## GLASS & MIRRORS

**Chelsea Glass Ltd**
www.chelseaglass.co.uk

## HOME ACCESSORIES

**Home Style App by Kelly Hoppen**
www.itunes.com
**Kelly Hoppen by Welton**
www.weltonlondon.com
KH home fragrance
**KH for Earth Couture**
www.earth-couture.com
Organic home fashion collection
**KH Home Design for QVC**
www.qvcuk.com
**The Yard, Kelly Hoppen Store**
www.kellyhoppenretail.com

## LEATHER

**Alma Leather**
www.almahome.co.uk
**Edelman Leather**
www.edelmanleather.com
**Moore and Giles**
www.mooreandgilesinc.com

## LIGHTING

**Bella Figura**
www.bella-figura.co.uk
**CTO Lighting**
www.ctolighting.co.uk
**Kevin Reilly Lighting**
www.kevinreillylighting.com
**Lutron EA Ltd**
http://europe.lutron.com
Lighting systems
**Mark Brazier-Jones**
www.brazier-jones.com

**Ochre** www.ochre.net
**Porta Romana**
www.portaromana.co.uk
**Robert Clift Ltd**
www.robertcliftlighting.co.uk
Lighting designer
**Spina Design**
www.spinadesign.co.uk

## TELEVISION & SOUND

**N-Tegra (UK) Ltd** www.n-tegra.co.uk
**Opus Technologies** www.opus.eu

## WALLS

**Architectural Textiles**
www.architecturaltextiles.co.uk
Wallpaper and wall coverings
**Graham & Brown**
www.grahambrown.com/uk
KH wallpaper and wall art
**KH Paint**
www.kellyhoppenretail.com
**Polidori Barbera Design**
www.polidori-barbera.com
Specialist plaster wall finishes

## WINDOWS

**A&H Brass** www.aandhbrass.co.uk
Metalwork
**The Bradley Collection**
www.bradleycollection.co.uk
Poles and finials
**Kelly Hoppen Shutters**
www.kellyhoppenshutters.com
**McKinney & Co Ltd**
www.mckinney.co.uk
Poles and finials
**Shutterly Fabulous**
www.shutterlyfabulous.co.uk
Kelly Hoppen shutter collection
**Silent Gliss Ltd**
www.silentgliss.co.uk
Track systems and drapery

## FEATURED ARCHITECTS

**AEW Architects**
www.aewarchitects.com
**Brod Wight Architects**
www.brodwight.co.uk
**Duggan Morris Architects Ltd**
www.dugganmorrisarchitects.com
**Gérard Ravello** +33 450 211 565
**JKW Design** www.jkwdesign.co.uk
**Michael McCaffery Architect**
+1 212 227 1650

## ARTWORK CREDITS

p15 *Island and Torii Gate* © Josef Hoflehner/courtesy Michael Hoppen Gallery p34 top and p143 © Peter Beard/courtesy of the Peter Beard Studio p40, p52, and p90 top Desiree Dolron p43 *Jessica in Lace Dress* by Louise Bobbe p44 right (left to right) *Rosa meinivoz "Summer's Kiss"* © 1996, *Rosa "Black Beauty"* © 1998, *Tulipa "Maureen"* © 1997 all by Ron van Dongen p51 left *For Issey Miyake* by Sarah Moon p51 right and p137 *Topsy Turvy* by Daniel Kelly p53 left *Kelly Hoppen* by Amelia Troubridge p55 bottom left (top shelf) *Oasis* by Gered Mankowitz © Bowstir Ltd 2010/mankowitz.com/courtesy of Richard Goodall Gallery p55 bottom left (middle shelf) © David Hum/courtesy of Richard Goodall Gallery p63 and p96 top left *Jibby Beane* © Nadav Kander p77 *Rosa "Ferreus"* © Ron van Dongen/courtesy Michael Hoppen Gallery p90 bottom and p141 top © AMC at Colour Gallery 2009 p94 *I am not a Geisha* by Daniel Kelly p95 *Duffy* © Duffy Archive Ltd p111 © Nobuyoshi Araki/courtesy of Taka Ishii Gallery, Tokyo p159 *Brigitte Bardot* © Terry O'Neill/courtesy of Richard Goodall Gallery p165 top *Central Park South, 1998* by Jason Langer p176 (top artwork) and p192 bottom right (top artwork) from the *Butterfly Book* series by Julie Cockburn p176 (bottom artwork) and p192 bottom right (bottom artwork) from the *Playboy* series by Julie Cockburn p183 top and bottom right (from left to right) *Rosa "Fantasy"* © 1996, *Rosa meinivoz "Summer's Kiss"* © 1996, *Rosa "Black Beauty"* © 1998, *Tulipa "Maureen"* © 1997 all by Ron van Dongen p200 and p201 bottom right *Swimmer, Cannes, France, 1993* © Nadav Kander.